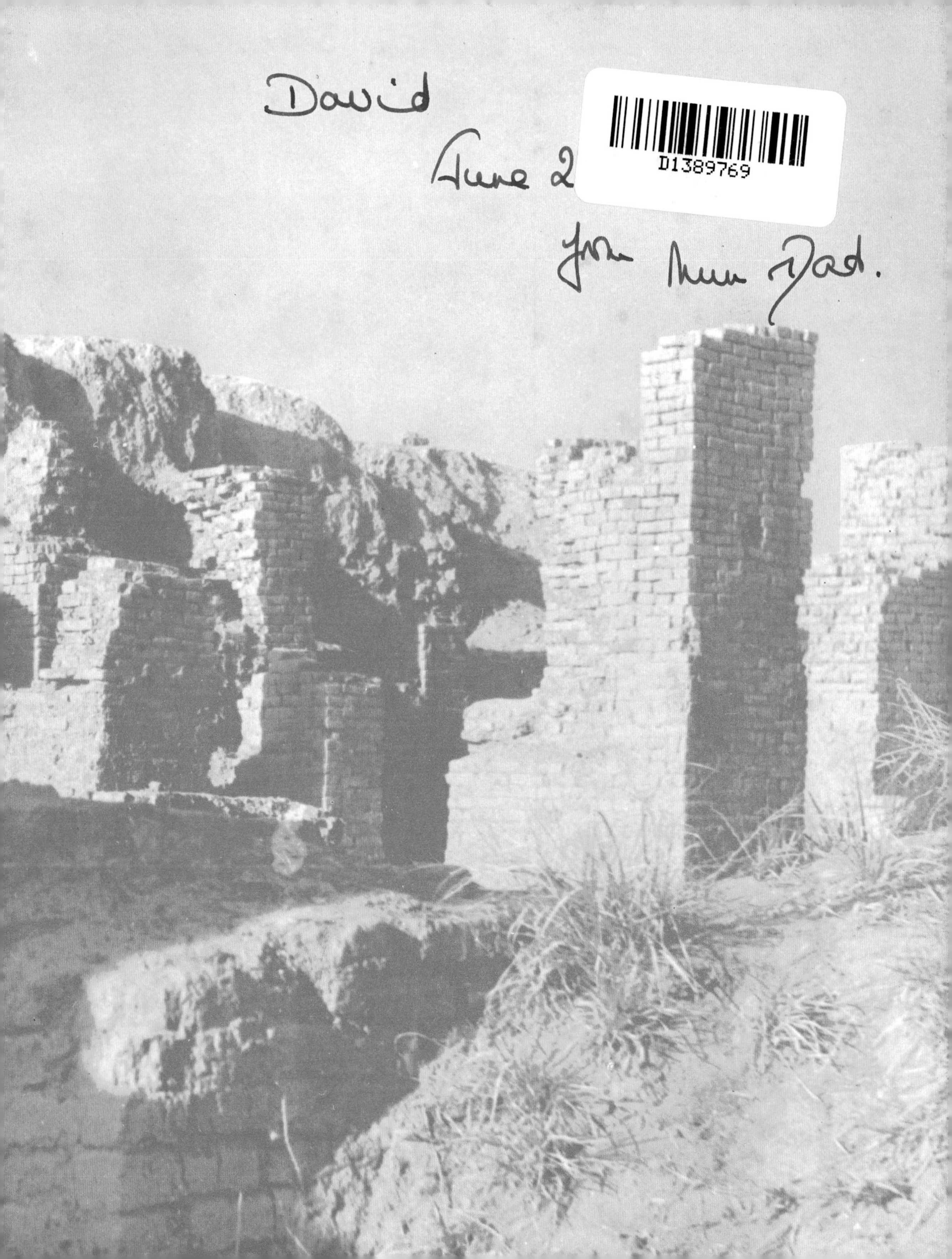

David

June 2

from Mum Dad.

Babylon

The World of Babylon

Nineveh and Assyria

Text by **Charles Seignobos**
Translated by David Macrae

Editions Minerva

Contents

© Editions Minerva, S.A., Genève, 1975
Printer, Industria Gráfica, S.A.
Tuset, 19   Barcelona · San Vicente dels Horts   1975
Depósito legal B. 39-1975
Printed in Spain

Ruins of the ancient city of Nimrud.

1. The ancient empires of Chaldea and Assyria

The landscape

High in the snow-covered mountains of Armenia lie the sources of two great rivers, the Euphrates and the Tigris, which flow, at first, in opposite directions and eventually meet as they enter the sea.

At first, the Euphrates is a gushing torrent, leaping from one waterfall to the next; then it runs along the bottom of a deep ravine, between sheer rock walls or great piles of fallen boulders. It heads west, later turning south, towards the Mediterranean. Navigation is quite out of the question in the upper reaches of the river, because of the rapid, turbulent currents; in order to cross it, the inhabitants lie flat on small craft which consist of wineskins made out of sheep's hides, attached to wooden frames.

Once it has left the mountains, the Euphrates becomes a placid river, about 100-130 yards wide, flowing slowly across a vast, arid plain. It makes a sharp turn to the east, and heads for its final destination, the Persian Gulf. The landscape through which it passes is a virtual desert, containing a few rather scant rivers, the main one being the Khabur, which are almost dry during the summer. Some of its water is lost on the way across the plain, where it forms huge marshes, covered with forests of reeds; what remains in a mere river of mud, inching its way painfully forward, and leaving a long trail of yellowish water across the sand.

The Tigris is no more than two-thirds the length of the Euphrates, but is deeper, faster and fuller. It has three sources, known as the *three lakes*, which lie very close to one of the branches of the Euphrates; indeed, there is only the thickness of a mountain between them. It begins as a turbulent, foaming stream at the bottom of sheer ravines, and then becomes a river, a hundred yards wide, racing along past tall grey cliffs. It emerges from the mountains into a vast plain, sloping towards the south, where it is fed by big rivers which, like it, have their source high in the mountains and are always well filled; it therefore flows fast and abundantly all the year round. Eventually it grows to a width of more than 200 yards, becoming navigable for shallow-draft boats from Mossul and for steamers from Baghdad.

Continuing its south-easterly course, it reaches the low-lying and perfectly flat plain in which the Euphrates is situated. At Bahgdad, the two rivers are only a few miles apart; indeed, through the canals, their waters can actually mingle. They run parallel for about 25 miles and then diverge, not meeting again until their final confluence, 200 miles further on, in the midst of marshy country, when they form a single, sand-laden river, more than 500 yards wide, emptying sluggishly into the Persian Gulf.

At one time, when the hinterland was much closer to the sea than it is today, the Tigris and the Euphrates used to have separate mouths; but the silt carried down to the sea by the two rivers gradually filled in the offshore parts of the Gulf. Even today, the coastline is moving further out to sea at a rate of something like half a mile every 36 years.

The great low-lying plain, barely above sea-level, in which the Tigris and the Euphrates meet, forms the area known as Chaldaea. The

Left: god and sacred flower, early Chaldaean stele (Paris, Louvre). Above: date-palms near Baghdad.

long strip of land between the parallel sections of the rivers used to be called *Mesopotamia* (Greek for *between the rivers*); the Arabs called it *El-Djezireh* (the island).

Chaldaea and Mesopotamia were a homogeneous plain, made up entirely of a rich yellowish soil deposited by the rivers: it lacked rocks or relief of any sort.

The climate is extraordinarily dry; apart from the torrential winter rains, which last for only a few days, there is only a remote chance of rain throughout the rest of the year.

The winds, which sweep unimpeded across the land, are quite fierce. In winter, the cold north wind brings icy mountain air down on to the plain; frost occurs on January mornings; the marshes become covered with a thin layer of ice which melts during the day; the camels are sometimes so stiff from the cold that they are barely able to move; in fact, their Arab riders have been known to become so numb that they fall from the saddle.

As early as April, the heat is very uncomfortable, and in summer it is simply overpowering,

7

rising to 110 and even 120 degrees in the shade. There is no question of staying out of doors in the middle of the day; the people seek relief from the heat inside darkened rooms, like cellars, from which they emerge in the evening. At night, many of them sleep outside their houses; but even the nights are stiflingly hot. For months on end, there is not a drop of rain; the south-east wind, which comes off the sea, loses all its moisture as it passes over the deserts, and brings no rain; however, it does fill the air with a fine, sandy dust which lines the membranes of the nose and throat.

Like Egypt, Chaldaea is surrounded by a huge desert of sand, and would itself be a desert, were it not for the Euphrates and the Tigris. Without them, the whole area would be uninhabitable. In the distant past, these two rivers deposited the region's soil, which they now fertilize with their life-giving water.

In spring of each year, when the mountain snows melt, the two rivers suddenly swell and flood the surrounding countryside; two or three weeks later the waters recede, leaving swamps which the blazing sun quickly dries out.

As the area is now governed by incompetent Turks, these floods do only harm. The fast-flowing Tigris erodes the land; the Euphrates spills over its low right bank, flooding vast areas to the west, creating enormous swamps, covered with forests of reeds, which promote the spread of fever through the whole region. When the floods have subsided, and the earth has dried out, all that is left is a foul black mud, baked into cracked shapes by the sun. Near the ruins of Babylon, the only people to be seen today are a few fever-stricken wretches or Bed-

Left: Chaldaean art-work, pyramid of Manishtusu (Paris, Louvre). Above: Ruins of Ur, in Chaldaea.

ouin bandits from the desert, who roam the countryside looking for travellers to rob. In the swamps of the Euphrates, a few Arabs live in huts made of reeds and mud, built on low islands which they can leave only on flat-bottomed boats, along the narrow channels they make through the dense thickets of reeds.

This land, now a desert, used to be one of the most fertile places on earth. With a good water supply, the soil of Chaldaea is incomparably fertile. Even now, the spring rains bring forth vast expanses of thick, tall grass, and cover the ground with a lush carpet of flowers. Layard, the British explorer, reported that his greyhounds used to disappear from sight into the tall grass, and come out later with gay

splashes of red, blue or yellow all over their bodies, depending on the color of the flowers which they had brushed against. Yet this splendor is short-lived: by May, the sun has reduced it all to a few dried stalks, covered with grey dust. Yet the inhabitants have it within their power to make this a fertile land; they simply have to irrigate it.

The Chaldeans of ancient times had built dikes to hold back the floods, and dug reservoirs to store the water, together with canals to carry it to the plains. They thereby produced some astonishing harvests, particularly of grains. Wheat grows naturally in this area, like a type of wild grass. In ancient times, each plant used to yield between 200 and 300 grains; it had extraordinarily broad leaves, and grew so fast that it had to be harvested promptly or left for the cattle to graze on. Sorghum and sesame plants grew almost to the size of bushes. Herodotus, who had himself visited Chaldaea, said of it: "I shall not even say how high the sorghum and sesame grow, because I know that anyone who has not actually been to the country of Babylon would certainly not believe me."

The only trees in Chaldaea were the palm-

Huge herds of cattle and sheep used to graze on the grasslands. Geese and ducks lived along the rivers and canals; the waters abounded with carp and barbel.

For thirty centuries, this land supported one of the largest population groups in the world.

The region to the north of Chaldaea, upstream along the Tigris, as far as the mountains to the North and East, comprised Assyria. This also was a plain, but one with a slightly undulating surface, interrupted by the occasional chain of rocky, grey hills.

The soil, consisting of sand or rock, was naturally barren and dry, but layers of fertile ground were to be found along the river banks, and the sand itself could be made fertile by irrigation. Like the Chaldaeans, the Assyrians made fields and orchards by bringing water from the rivers into the desert.

The lower part of Assyria has more or less the same hot, dry climate as Chaldaea, and, like it, grew wheat and grains, but had no trees.

In the upland regions, especially in the valleys formed by the tributaries of the Tigris, which reach as far as the foot of the high, snow-covered mountains, the winter is more severe than in Chaldaea; for three months, there is heavy rain, and sometimes even snow. Spring is characterized by heavy dew on the ground and by occasional, violent thunderstorms. Summer is less oppressive; the heat is frightful during the day, but the nights are less hot and the air is less dry.

Walnut- and plane-trees, oaks and sycamores all grow in these regions.

Unlike Chaldaea, Assyria has stone-quarries, soft sandstone, alabaster which can

trees along the rivers and canals, and the orange-trees and certain types of fruit-trees which grew in orchards. Apart from providing dates, however, the palm-trees supplied a host of other needs; from them, the inhabitants used to make a sort of bread, a sort of wine, vinegar, a sort of sugar, and threads from which fabrics were woven. Palm-trunks were used as beams, while blacksmiths used date-stones to heat their furnaces and farmers used them to feed their cattle. There was a Persian song of the period which listed three hundred and sixty uses for the palm-tree.

easily be cut up into sections, and marble; in the northeastern mountains, iron, lead, copper and silver are mined.

Wild animals roamed the deserts at will; on the plains there were lions, leopards, gazelles, ostriches, partridges, buffalo, partridge, wild donkeys, greyhounds and hedgehogs; on higher ground, there were bears, deer and ibex. Today, almost all of these animals are rare.

The ancient cities of Chaldaea

The Chaldaean priests claimed that their country had been governed by kings for more than thirty thousand years; one of these kings was supposed to have reigned for two thousand seven hundred years. This is obviously a fable; but it is certainly true that there were some very ancient kingdoms in the plain of the Euphrates, some of them even older than the kingdom of Egypt.

More than three thousand years before the Christian era, the inhabitants of Chaldaea knew how to grow wheat, make statues out of baked clay, and work with metals; they already had a form of writing and were able to draw; they built towns and monuments.

These cities were built of unbaked bricks; when they collapsed, they formed mounds of earth, large numbers of which are to be seen dotted about the plain of the Euphrates. Various explorers decided it might be worth while to dig into these hills of clay, and by so doing they discovered a dozen or more lost cities: in the lower part of the Euphrates, Ur, Eridu, Uruk, Larsa, Sirtella; further upstream, between the Tigris and the Euphrates, Nippur, Sippar, Akkad, Babilu. Our knowledge of these cities and their history is based entirely on these excavations.

Each city worshipped its own special god and had a temple built in its name. The priest of the temple was, at the same time, the king of the city. Some of these priest-kings subjugated the neighboring cities and united part of Chaldaea into a single kingdom. One of the oldest such kingdoms, Urea, previously bore the title of "king of Ur, king of Sumer and Akkad".

For more than two thousand years, Chaldaea saw a succession of kings, of whom we know nothing, often not even their name. During this long period, the country was twice conquered by foreign kings who founded new dynasties. The first time, about the XXIII century, the conquerors were the kings of Elam, from the east; they took back with them the statue of the goddess Nana, which they had seized from the temple of Uruk. The second time, about the XVI century, it was the kings of a warlike people from the northern mountains, the area now inhabited by the Kurds, who overran Chaldaea. After several generations, these invaders merged with the original inhabitants, while the population of Chaldaea kept their own language, religion and customs.

Among all of these Chaldeans kings, two or three are better known, because fairly long inscriptions have been found, giving a more detailed picture of their reign.

In 1878, at Sirtella, a French explorer unearthed the ruins of a palace 170 feet long, and 100 wide, built on a huge embankment 38 feet high. The towers are made of bricks ce-

mented together with tar; each brick bears the name of King Gudea, who ordered the building of the palace. Two tombs and the foundations of a temple to the god Nin-Girsu were discovered nearby.

The courtyard of the palace was found to contain nine big statues made of black stone, and a number of statuettes made of alabaster, ivory and bronze; however, the heads had been knocked off all the statues. The biggest one showed King Gudea, with his hands joined, dressed in long robes, sitting on a throne. An inscription carved on his robes says what he had done: he built the temple to the god Nin-Girsu, and sent a ship a long way off to find the black stone which was used to make the statues. Another statue shows King Gudea sitting, with the plan for a temple with six doors spread out across his lap: this was the temple to Nin-Girsu.

King Sargon reigned in Akkad. The story was that his mother had given birth to him in secret, for fear that his uncle might have him killed; she had laid him in a reed basket coated with tar and set him adrift on the Euphrates. A laborer, who happened to be filling his bucket from the river, rescued the child and raised him as his own son. Sargon, who was protected by the goddess Ishtar, eventually became king of Agade. Then he conquered the whole of Chaldaea and Elam, all the way to the Mediterranean.

He rebuilt the temple of Akkad and recorded the current state of knowledge of astrology, magic and grammar on stone tablets. It was thought that these tablets had all been assembled in the city of Erech (the Biblical form of the

name Uruk), which was known as the *city of books*.

In the XVII century, the whole of Chaldaea became united under the reign of King Hammurabi, the king of Babylon. He built two great temples in Babylon, and restored the temples in other cities. He also built a series of enormous dikes to protect the plain against floods, and dug a network of irrigation channels. In an inscription, the following words are attributed to him: "The gods have ordained that I should govern the peoples of Sumer and Akkad, and have filled my hands with the tributes they have paid to me. I built the Hammurabi canal, which is such a boon to the inhabitants of Chaldaea; I have sent the branches of the canal across the barren plains of the desert, so as so provide the peoples of Sumer and Akkad with unending supplies of water; I have made the desert bloom, for the happiness of all who live there."

The kingdom of Assyria

The Tigris valley to the north of Chaldaea was inhabited by a people belonging to the same race as the Chaldaeans, but poorer and much more warlike. Their main city stood on the banks of the Tigris, near the temple to the

Left: bronze statuette of Gudea. (Louvre). Right: the "small seated statue" of Gudea. (Louvre).

15

Statuette of goddess, from Samara. (Baghdad Museum). Right: alabaster statuette of woman, from Ur. (Baghdad Museum).

Left: demon holding a bird, Sumer. (Louvre). Right: ruins of the Ziggurat and the city of Ur. Stairs leading to the main entrance of the Ziggurat.

Left: the bases of statues dating from about 2,500 B.C. (Louvre). Above: inscriptions on a brick wall, at Ur. Opposite: outside view of the Ziggurat of Ur.

god Ashur, and it was named Ashur, or El-Assar, after that same god. This was the *Assyrian* people.

The Assyrians obeyed the high-priest of their god Ashur, who was both priest and king at the same time. For many years, these priest-kings owed allegiance to the great king of Babylon. Then they became independent, subjugated the surrounding areas and assumed the title of king. They set up an army of foot-soldiers, called themselves *king of legions*, and began to wage war on all their neighbors. They even conquered Babylon and forced the kings of Chaldaea to pay tribute to them.

The most famous of these Assyrian conquerors is Tiglath Pileser, who reigned in the XII century. He left an account of his victories in an inscription, seven hundred lines long, which was found in the ruins of his capital. This is what he had to say about himself: "I am Tiglath Pileser, the mighty king, the king of the invincible legions, the king of the four corners of the earth, the prince of princes, lord of lords, king of kings, the supreme monarch ... the conqueror, the giant who, like a great river bursting its banks, overruns enemy countries. Through the favor of god Ashur, I have no rivals, I am the master of all the enemies of Ashur". This is followed by a description of the king's expeditions.

"At the beginning of my reign, I defeated 20,000 Mushku and their five kings, who, for the past fifty years, had been levying a tribute which really belonged to Ashur, my master. No other king dared to oppose them; they had invaded the Assyrian province of Kummuh. I prayed to Ashur, my master, and assembled my war-chariots and soldiers ... I routed the en-

emy completely, so that their bodies were strewn over both mountain tops and ravines; I cut off their heads and displayed them on the battlements of their cities, I returned home with a huge amount of loot. The 6,000 men of the enemy force who had escaped death at the hands of my army, came and kissed my feet; I took them prisoner, and led them back into Assyria.''

Tiglath Pileser left similar accounts of all his other campaigns. In the west, he invaded Kummuh, burnt down the cities and pursued the inhabitants to their fortresses beyond the Tigris. A king from a nearby country who had come to their aid was seized, along with his sons, daughters, statues of gods and ingots of gold and silver; his palace and city were both burned to the ground. Tiglath Pileser showed his gratitude by offering a bronze vase to his god Ashur.

In another campaign, he invaded the region in which the sources of the Tigris are situated. "The god Ashur ordered me to begin marching; I assembled my chariots and my warriors, and set off into an impenetrable terrain, passing between mountain peaks as sharp as a dagger, where there was no room for my chariots to pass. I left my chariots down in the plain and scaled the mountains . . . I left ruins behind me everywhere, and punished the enemy armies; I occupied their cities, carried off their gods, I took them into captivity along with their treasures, I burnt their cities to the ground, demolished them and then gave thanks to the lord god Ashur''.

Next came Armenia. The king described his exploits thus: "I crossed inaccessible mountains, high mountain passes where no king had ever led his troops, steep rocky paths, dense undergrowth''. Twenty-three kings gathered to repel the invader, but they were routed, and had to abandon one hundred and twenty war chariots. The Assyrians laid siege to the fortresses, massacred their garrisons and the captured the kings alive. Tiglath Pileser released them from captivity, but imposed on them a tribute of 1,200 horses and 2,000 oxen, and took away their sons as hostages.

He also waged war on the peoples of Syria and conquered the northern part of Chaldaea. It was at this point, during the fifth year of his reign, that he prepared the inscription which gives such a full account of his campaigns. In it, he also describes how he went hunting. "With the protection of my gods, while I was in the desert, I killed four male buffalo of extraordinary size and strength; I killed them with my bow, my iron sword and my lance, and brought their hides and horns back to my city of Ashur. Another time, I killed ten big elephants near the source of the Khabur, and brought their hides and tusks back to Ashur; I also caught some live elephants. On one occasion, I killed a hundred and twenty lions."

Finally, he tells how he repaired the temples, rebuilt statues and roofs; he replaced the old doors by new ones made of wood from trees cut down in conquered lands. He even uprooted trees which he later tried to replant in his own country.

The kingdom of Ashur, at that time, stretched from Lebanon in the west to beyond the Euphrates in the east, as far as the Armenian mountains and the Black Sea in the north, and the Persian Gulf in the south. But the sub-

Sa-ud, grandson of Lugalkisalsi, king of Uruk (Louvre). Right: fragment of a statue of Gudea (Louvre).

jugated peoples soon rose against their rulers. It is unlikely that the empire lasted until the death of Tiglath Pileser.

Ninus and Semiramis

A legend which the Greeks used to find enthralling was the story of the fabulous adventures of Ninus, king of Assyria, and Semiramis, queen of Babylon.

Ninus, the son of Belus, was said to have been the first king of Assyria. Eager to make vast conquests for himself, he created an army of stalwart men and set off on his campaigns. First, he subdued Chaldaea, seized the king and his children and had them executed; then he turned to Armenia, plundered it and won the loyalty of its king; then the king of Media was conquered, seized and crucified. As a result of these wars, which lasted seventeen years, Ninus conquered the whole of Asia, as far as India. He then decided that he should have a fitting capital for such an empire, and built Nineveh.

The inhabitants of Bactria, to the west of India, having resisted his advance, he set out again, this time with one million seven hundred thousand foot soldiers, two hundred thousand on horseback and ten thousand chariots armed with scythes in order to subdue Bactria; it was during this war that he came to know Semiramis.

Semiramis was the daughter of a goddess who was worshipped at Ascalon in Syria, and who was said to have the head of a woman on the body of a fish. After the girl's birth, her mother had left her stranded in the desert

Family picture of king Ur-Vina, Chaldaea; about 3,000 B.C. (Louvre).

among the rocks. However, she was discovered by some doves whose nests were nearby and who looked after the abandoned child; they covered her with their wings to keep her warm, bringing her milk in their bills from a sheep-pen, and feeding it into her mouth, drop by drop; later, they stole cheese for her to eat. Eventually, the shepherds noticed the doves' activity, followed them and discovered a superb young girl, nestling among the boulders. They took her with them to the official in charge of Ninus' domains, who adopted her and named her Semiramis (the Syrian for dove).

When she grew up, Semiramis married a governor and went with him when he set off, in Ninus' army, to fight the Bactrians. At one point, they were laying siege to a fortress where the enemy king had taken refuge. Ninus' troops were facing stiff resistance; Semiramis, dis-guised as a soldier, scaled the ramparts and en-abled the attacking force to enter the city. Ninus was so enchanted by her bravery that he mar-ried her, after which her husband hanged him-self in despair.

Shortly afterwards, Ninus died, and was bur-ied underneath a pyramid 3,000 feet high. Semiramis was his successor. She built a capital city for herself on the lower Euphrates which was even more splendid than Nineveh: that city was Babylon. Around it she built ramparts 40 miles long, wide enough to accomodate six cha-riots abreast; she erected a dam across the Eu-phrates and built a huge temple. She then vis-ited the different regions of her far-flung empire, building roads and cities, cutting passes through the mountains and erecting monu-ments in honor of her dead generals. She went

27

to Egypt and consulted the oracle of Amon, which told her that she would disappear miraculously and be venerated as a goddess. She also conquered Ethiopia.

Hoping to win glory as a great conqueror, she set off on an expedition to India and crossed the Indus; but the king of India used his overwhelming elephant-power to repel her advance. After this setback, she remained confined to her own kingdom, and once more began building monuments. (Later on, the inhabitants of Asia were to attribute to Semiramis every large monumental building). It was said that she had placed an inscription describing her exploits at the very limits of the inhabited world, in the middle of the steppes near the Aral Sea: "Nature has given me the body of a woman, but my deeds have made me the equal of the bravest of men."

On learning that her son Ninyas was conspiring to bring about her downfall, she chose to abdicate in his favor rather than punish him. Then she was turned into a dove and flew away. The Assyrians worshipped her as a goddess in the form of a dove.

Chaldaean traditions

The Chaldaeans had other traditions.

According to one story, the god Bel, angered by the crimes of men, had firmly decided to punish them. But another god warned the king Xisuthros, and told him: "Build a big ship for yourself and your kinfolk, and put on board creatures from each species, for I am going to destroy all living things." Xisuthros built a ship, which he coated with tar; he loaded his gold and silver on board; then his family and servants; and, lastly, a variety of animals, both wild and domestic; after which, he closed the door.

Immediately, the rain began to fall in torrents and the sky darkened. The storm lasted six days and seven nights; the whole country was flooded and all living things were drowned.

On the seventh day the rains stopped and the wind slackened. Xisuthros opened the window of his ship; he saw corpses floating all around, like so many tree-trunks, and burst into tears. Yet the water was receding; and eventually the boat ran aground on the top of a high mountain in Armenia. Xisuthros waited for six days, and then released a dove, which later returned to the boat as it could find nowhere to land. Xisuthros then released a crow; but the crow saw the corpses floating on the water, ate them and never returned. Eventually, the water level fell; Xisuthros opened the ark; his companions went down into Chaldaea and founded Babylon.

Their descendants multiplied in number until they were a great and powerful nation. They then began to build a tower which was meant to reach up into the sky; and they did, in fact, build a gigantic tower, called the *Tower of Babel*. It had already come quite close to heaven when the gods, irritated by the insolence of men, stopped the whole venture. Until that moment, the workers had all spoken the same language; one day, they noticed that they could no longer understand each other, as the gods had made them speak different languages. All work promptly came to a halt, and the Tower of Babel remained unfinished. Having been quite

unable, since the *confusion of tongues*, to communicate with each other, all those involved scattered in many directions and went off to people the world.

Another story often told was that of the adventures of Nimrud, the great hunter. He was a fearsome warrior, who subdued the whole of Chaldaea and Assyria and built Nineveh. He also was thought to have gone mad with pride and been so bold as to declare war on the gods. He shot an arrow into the sky, hoping to transfix a divinity, but the arrow fell back on him and killed him. According to an Arab legend, Nimrud died while trying to climb into the sky on the wings of an eagle. Even today, in Chaldaea, his name is used to designate a tower, now in ruins, which stands on a mound, on the site of the ancient city of Ur: it is known as the Tower of Nimrud.

Left: statuette of a goddess (Baghdad Museum). Right: the same subject, statuette from Susa (Louvre).

Below: votive offering of Hammurabi, about 2,000 B.C. (Louvre).

31

Votive tablet depicting religious scene, from the region of Ur. (Baghdad Museum).

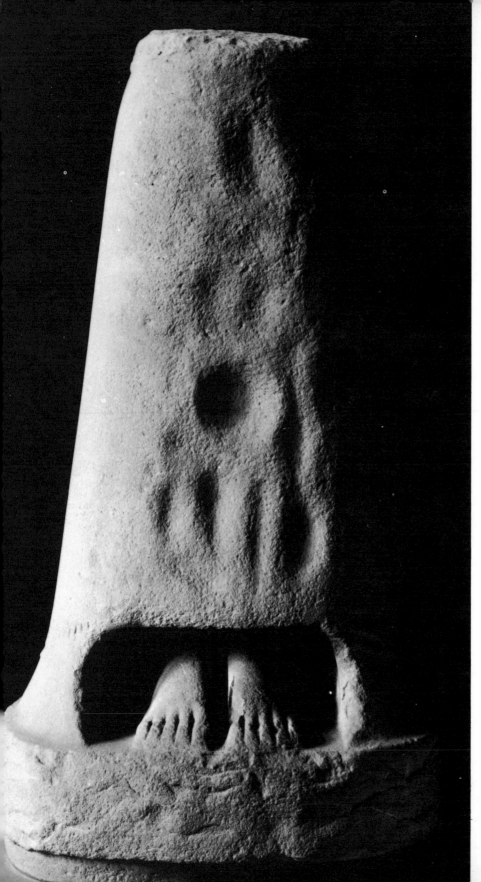

Left: early Chaldaean statuette (Louvre). Right: terra cotta bas-relief, about 1,800 B.C. (Baghdad Museum).

Left: bas-relief showing a king presenting his daughter to the goddess Nanna (Louvre). Above: the sun-god dictating his laws to Hammurabi. (Louvre).

Susa: bronze model of a ritual ceremony held at sunrise (Louvre). Below: the walls of Nineveh.

2. Nineveh

The city

While Ashur was still the capital of Assyria, there was a fortified city, a long way upstream on the Tigris, called Nineveh. It was situated at the river's edge, at the point where it becomes navigable, only a few miles from the mountains, and at the entrance to one of the world's most vast and fertile plains.

One of the early kings of Ashur had built a temple to the goddess Ishtar on this site; another king built a palace there in about the XIII century. Gradually, Nineveh became the chief city of the kingdom, and the capital city of the Assyrian people. The kings abondoned Ashur and moved their seat to Nineveh, where they built new palaces, either in or around the city. Today's visitor will notice that the plain in this region is strewn with mounds of earth, which conceal the ruins of these palaces.

Later, in the XII century, king Sennacherib greatly enlarged Nineveh and enhanced its beauty. He built new fortifications, surrounded by a moat; the total perimeter was said to be about 50 miles around, containing not just houses and other buildings, but also fields. The fortifications were 50 feet thick and 160 feet high. The earlier palace, built right at the water's edge, had been undermined by floods, so badly, in fact, that the walls of the embankment had been breached. Sennacherib had the course of the Tigris altered, the breach filled in and the palace itself demolished. In its place, a new, much bigger palace was built. Its beams were made of cedar, sandalwood, ebony and pistachio-wood; its walls were covered with bas-reliefs and inscriptions. It was surrounded by

Statue of woman, Nineveh (British Museum).

39

ramparts with battlements and fortified gates. It covered an area of five acres. Nearby, he erected a huge building of marble, with cedar beams; it had ornate doors decorates with colossal bulls and lions: this was known as the *house of tributes*. It served as a storage place for the accumulated gold, silver and other valuable objects taken from vanquished peoples.

Sometimes, the Tigris overflowed its banks and reached right into the middle of the city; Sennacherib built brick wharves which had parapets made of stone blocks. He also altered the irregular alinement of the buildings in the old city, making the arrangement of streets rectangular.

Sennacherib kept the fountains of Nineveh full and provided enough water to irrigate the surrounding land by bringing water from two mountain rivers by means of canals. The plain around the city blossomed with an abundance of wheat, barley and vines.

Nineveh was also a trading center, to which all the products of neighboring countries were transported by boat on the Tigris or by caravan through the mountains. For two centuries, it was the greatest city in the world.

The Assyrians

For many years, the whole of the territory bordering on the Tigris, as far as Chaldaea, had been one single kingdom. The Assyrians who lived there were a ferocious warlike people, with well organized infantry and cavalry.

The foot soldiers wore a cuirass of leather panels which covered their body, while their head was protected by a metal helmet with a crest on top; when in battle, they used a round shield. Their weapons were a highly curved bow from which they shot short arrows, a lance which also served as a javelin, and a small sword which they used only rarely.

The cavalry rode small broad-tailed horses,

Left: fragment of glazed brick panel, Nineveh (Baghdad Museum). Right: head of horse, about 1,000 B.C.

with neither stirrups nor saddle, though they sometimes laid a small rug over the horse's back. Like the infantry, their main weapon was the bow and the lance.

The rich, and, on most occasions, the king, went into battle standing up on a very light, two-wheeled chariot, open at the back only, which was drawn by a pair of richly caparisoned horses.

While on a campaign, the Assyrians used to build earthwork fortifications around their camp, and put up canvas tents supported by poles. An Assyrian bas-relief shows soldiers inside their tents: one of them is making his bed, while another is cooking and a third is arranging some things on a little table.

When laying siege to fortresses, the Assyrians did not merely shoot arrows and rocks against the defenders, set fire to the gates or scale the outer walls on ladders. They also had machines: the ram and the mobile tower. The ram was a huge suspended beam, usually ending in a monster's head, which they used to swing to und fro, so that the head would smash into the base of the ramparts and open a breach in the wall. The mobile tower was a square wooden tower, standing on a wheeled platform, and high enough to look over the top of the ramparts; warriors were sent up inside, the tower was rolled forward to the wall of the besieged city, and the warriors stationed inside would shoot arrows and hurl stones down at the defenders.

The Assyrians were also able to make underground passages which enabled their demolition squads to reach their target—the enemy ramparts—under cover.

Every spring, the king of Assyria commanded his troops to assemble and set off on an expedition; they would invade a region and lay waste everything in their path. They often met with resistance, but, being better organized than most of their adversaries, usually won. When the battle was over, they chopped the heads off the dead and put the prisoners in chains, often killing them, too. Then they laid siege to the capital city, looting everything within, if they succeeded in taking it: statues and sacred vases from the temples, furniture, clothes and carpets from private houses. They then set fire to the whole city and withdrew with their loot, leaving behind them an empty, shattered landscape.

They used to take back with them not only the warriors captured in battle, but also workers, women, girls and boys; they were made to accompany the victorious army back to Assyria, mingled with the herds of cattle, the goats and sheep, and chariots and camels all loaded down with furniture, fabrics, sacks of grain and fruit. On their return, the king and the warriors shared out the booty and the captives among themselves.

Being a hunter and warrior himself, the king usually commanded the army in person. He rode a war-chariot and was armed with a bow. In peace-time, he lived in a palace, clad in a richly embroidered robe and a very short cloak, wearing bracelets, necklaces and earrings, and with a diadem or a pointed tiara on his head. Two servants accompanied him, one carrying a parasol and the other a plumed fly-whisk.

The king was an absolute master who called himself the "shepherd of the peoples"; and, indeed, his subjects did obey him just like sheep following a shepherd. The popular belief was that the god Ashur had made him king to command the Assyrians and also to subdue the kings of other nations. In order not to invite a visit from the terrible Assyrian warriors, the kings of smaller neighboring peoples had to come to Nineveh and bow to the ground at the king's feet, declare allegiance to him and bring him gifts of gold, silver and precious fabrics. Those who refused were treated as insurgents; if they were captured, they were flayed alive, crucified or impaled.

Ashur-nasir-pal

The great expeditions began in the IX century during the reign of King Ashur-nasir-pal (885). Our description is based on the king's own account of them.

With his warriors and chariots, he set out from Nineveh and headed north up the Tigris, as far as the mountains of Armenia. The inhabitants fled to the mountain tops, which were "as sharp as the tip of a dagger, and which only the birds of the sky could reach". The Assyrians scaled the mountains, took 200 prisoners whom they then proceeded to massacre, and seized all the livestock. "The corpses were strewn, like autumn leaves, all over the mountains". The horrified peoples from neighboring regions hastened to prostrate themselves before the king and offer him gifts of horses, cattle and sheep. The army then took a dozen cities and sacked them. The Assyrians took the one fortress which did try to resist, and, on the king's orders, massacred all the defenders, chopped off their heads and hung their bodies on stakes; their chief was taken back in chains to Arbela (Arbailu) where he was flayed alive and displayed on the ramparts. Ashur-nasir-pal built a city, named after himself, in the conquered territory, and placed a statue bearing his inscription outside the city gates. Then, in the sweltering summer heat, he set off again, plundered and burnt twenty more villages and crossed the Tigris to demand tribute from the inhabitants of Kummuh.

At this moment, he learnt that the inhabitants of Suru, in Mesopotamia, had rebelled, killed their governor and proclaimed Ahiabab king. He promptly went there with his army; on hearing of his approach, the people became fearful and decided to beg for pardon. He himself relates the way he responded to their appeals: "I killed every other one of them and led the survivors into captivity; I built a pyramid outside the gates of the city, flayed alive some of the ringleaders and had them stretched out on that pyramid. Others were buried alive as part of the masonry, while others were impaled along the ramparts. I had many of them flayed alive in my presence, and then lined the walls with their skins. I made crowns with their heads and wreaths with their corpses. I took Ahiabab back to Nineveh, where I had him flayed and draped on the ramparts."

Then his armies withdrew, taking with them whole herds of slaves and cattle, and chariots loaded down with possessions "as numerous as the stars in the sky". The king had a colossal statue built in his palace. He was visited by another king, who had come to declare his allegiance, make gifts of gold and silver and offer his sons as hostages.

While resting from this expedition, he heard that an Assyrian governor, Hulai, had rebelled in the Tigris mountains. He promptly set off and overwhelmed the rebel fortresses. Some of the prisoners were executed, others had their eyes gouged out, their nose and ears chopped off; Hulai was flayed alive. His city was flattened, and, on the spot where it had once stood, Ashur-nasir-pal built a pyramid crowned by a statue of himself.

This was the record of Ashur-nasir-pal's first year as king; subsequent years were much the

same: in the second year, he went to war against the peoples of the Zagros Mountains; in the third, he invaded Armenia; in the fourth, he went on an expedition against the region of the Upper Tigris. Here is how Ashur-nasir-pal describes the seizure of a fortified city surrounded by two outer walls, high up on the crest of a mountain.

"With the aid of Ashur, my master, I attacked; for two whole days, I besieged the city from the east; showers of arrows were raining down upon the enemy, as dense as the hail sent by the god Raman. Eventually, my warriors fell upon the city like vultures and overpowered the enemy. I ordered eight hundred men massacred and had their heads cut off. With the corpses, I built a pyramid; I had another seven hundred crucified. The city was sacked and demolished." In another city, the king had the wrists chopped off two hundred prisoners.

Ashur-nasir-pal decided that he needed a new residence. The fortress of Calah (Calah is the Biblical name for Kalhu) stood at the confluence of the Zab and the Tigris, on an imposing site at the top of a hill between the two rivers; on the king's orders, the fortress was razed to the ground, and in its place was built a new city which, for many years, was used by the kings of Assyria as their residence. The palace was built on an embankment rising sheer out of

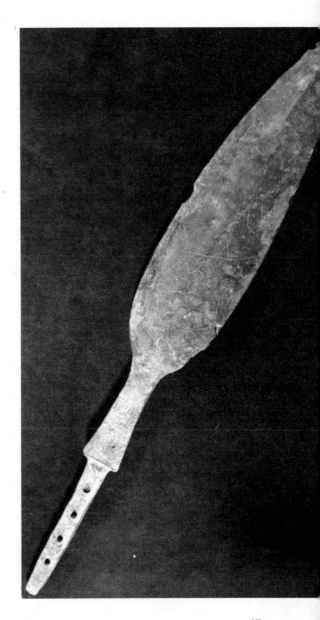

the Tigris; an enormous brick pyramid, near the temple to the god Ninib, dominated the whole landscape. Seen in the setting sun, against the bright colors of the Middle Eastern sky, Calah must really have seemed to the approaching traveller to be a city straight out of legend.

The palace contained the statue of the king, holding a scepter in one hand, and a scythe in the other. The following inscription was engraved on his chest: "Ashur-nasir-pal, great king, mighty king, king of legions, king of Assyria. He possesses the lands which stretch from the banks of the Tigris to Lebanon, he has extended his dominion over the great sea and over all countries, from the rising to the setting of the sun."

Ashur-nasir-pal reigned for twenty-five years, during which time he fought several more wars, and conquered the north of Syria.

His son Shalmaneser III, after five years spent subduing insurgent peoples, attacked the kings of Damascus and Israel and won a major battle in Syria. Unable to take Damascus, he cut all the trees for miles around. The king of Israel, Jehu, and the kings of Tyre and Sidon became apprehensive and declared their allegiance to the king of Assyria, sending him gold and silver ingots and vases. Shalmaneser also subjugated Babylon and Chaldaea. To commemorate his victories, he built a monument, the Nimrud obelisk, on which the vanquished kings are shown prostrate at his feet, followed by servants bringing tributes and leading in camels, horses, apes and elephants. The inscription also says that the king had been on thirty-one campaigns.

Sargon

For a whole century, the kings of Assyria continued these plunderous expeditions, using Calah as their base and capital city. One of them went as far as Media, another reached the Red Sea. Eventually, they were faced with a general revolt. But, about 745, Tiglath Pileser restored Assyrian domination, waging war for this purpose for more than fifteen years. He took Babylon and subdued Chaldaea, and later did the same with Damascus and Syria. The thousands of prisoners he took were used to build a new palace at Calah, which bore the following inscription: "I have subdued the nations and commanded men from both the mountains and the plains; I have overthrown kings and put my own lieutenants in their place."

The son of this great conqueror, Shalmaneser V, died during the fifth year of his reign, while his armies were laying siege to the capital of the people of Israel, Samaria. Sargon, his chief general, had the soldiers proclaim him king in the year 722. Eventually, Samaria fell to the Assyrians after a three-year siege, and was thoroughly sacked; Sargon kept for himself fifty war chariots and distributed the rest of his booty among his warriors. He took 27,280 prisoners, settling some of them in Calah and others in the area bordering on the Khabur. He replaced them by inhabitants of Chaldaea and Susiana, and also by Arabs whom he forcibly displaced from their homes.

Humbanigas, king of Susiana, had refused to recognize his sovereignty, and had actually invaded Babylonia. Sargon moved against him and repelled him.

Meanwhile, a part of Syria, led by the king of Hamath, had also risen up in rebellion. The Syrians were confident of support from an Egyptian army; but, before the Egyptians had time to arrive on the scene, Sargon struck into Syria, laid siege to the opposing forces, captured the king of Hamath and had him flayed alive. He then moved to intercept the king of Egypt, who had just joined forces with the king of Gaza. In an engagement at Rapihu, Sargon was victorious and the king of Gaza, together with his family, were taken prisoner and sent off to Assyria; the city was burned down, and 20,033 inhabitants led away into captivity. In order to punish the Arab chieftains who had fought against him, he attacked them, seized thirty war-chariots, killed 7,000 of their men and withdrew, leaving a governor in charge of the conquered area.

To the north of Assyria, in the mountains of Armenia, there was a powerful prince, Rusas, who had fortresses, an army and many war-chariots. On his urging, the vassals of the king of Assyria decided to rebel. Sargon acted to put down the rebellion, captured and burnt two towns and took their inhabitants into captivity in Syria. But he was unable to finish the job, as he had to leave suddenly to attend to troubles elsewhere, and could not return to the north until two years later. He spent this time in Syria and destroyed the city of Carchemish. The king of Egypt and an Arab queen sent him gifts of camels, incense, dogs and silver.

In Armenia, Sargon had a faithful ally, Aza, the king of the city of Van. Rusas and his chieftains captured Aza, killed him and left his corpse to be devoured by the wild beasts of the mountains. On hearing of this, Sargon promptly set out for the mountains; he seized one of the chieftains in question, and had him flayed alive at the precise spot where Aza had been cut down. He then appointed Ullusunu, Aza's brother, as king.

No sooner was Sargon's back turned, however, than Ullusunu allied himself with Rusas. The Assyrian army returned, and laid waste the whole country, like a swarm of locusts; the defeated Ullusuni threw himself at the feet of Sargon, who pardoned him. Nonetheless, the Assyrians moved vast numbers of inhabitants out of the surrounding lands.

Sargon then moved north-east, to put down an insurrection among the Medes. He captured their chief, destroyed their towns and deported 4,820 of their people to Syria.

Then he turned his attention once more towards Armenia. This time, Rusas was soundly defeated, his family, belongings and his entire cavalry being seized by the victors; he managed to escape alone on horseback into the mountains. All of his cities were sacked and burned. He was given refuge by another king, Urzana, whose territory was promptly invaded by Sargon; the capital city was stormed and looted, and 20,100 prisoners were taken, along with the statue of his god, a vast amount of booty and 682 mules. Rusas was overwhelmed by despair and took his own life.

Another Mede rebellion had taken place in the meantime. Sargon marched to suppress it, and 45 of the chiefs of the Medes came to recognize his sovereignty and pay a tribute of horses and cattle.

Then more trouble arose at the opposite end

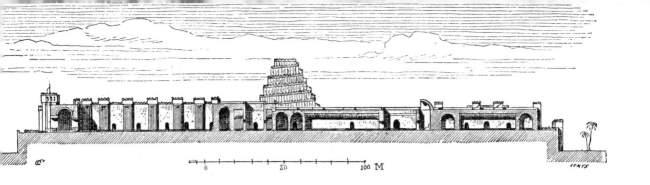

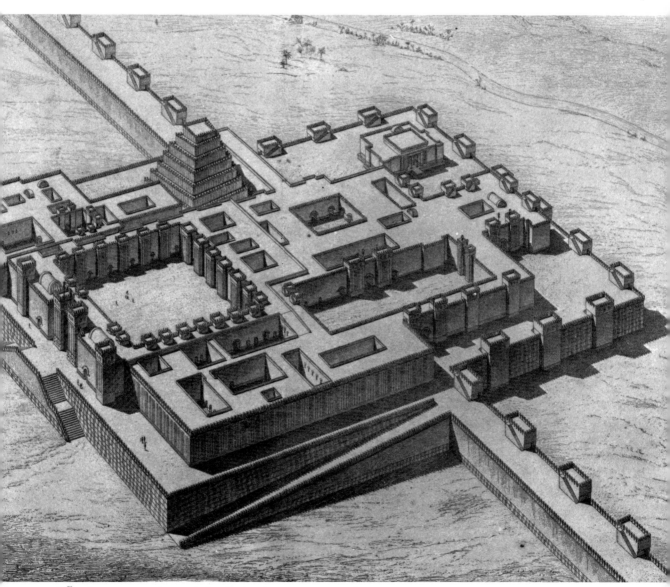

Façade, cross-section and view in depth of the palace of
Sargon at Khorsabad, reconstructed on the basis of actual remains.

51

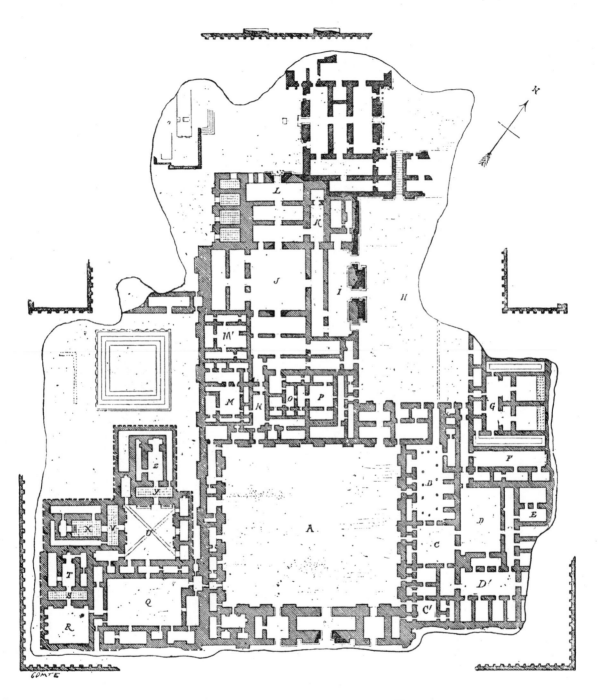

Above: layout of the palace of Sargon.
Right: bas-relief, Nineveh.

Left: bas-relief from the palace of Sargon: a protecting genie. Above and below: reconstruction of two bas-reliefs, showing the siege of Damascus and a king gouging out the eyes of a prisoner.

The god Ninib strangling a lion. He was regarded as the ancestor of the kings of Assyria. This bas-relief once formed part of the decor of the throne room in the palace of Sargon (Louvre). Right: statuettes of women, back view (Louvre).

of the empire, in the west, on the Asia Minor border. A king who was loyal to the Assyrians had just been dethroned by his son; Sargon took the usurper prisoner and installed a governor in his place. He then proceeded south to Ashdod, in the land of the Philistines. The people had refused to pay their tributes, had expelled their king and replaced him by a usurper; also, they had dug a deep moat around the city and filled it with water. On the arrival of the Assyrian army, the rebel king fled to Egypt. Sargon took the town, deported its inhabitants, whose place was taken by prisoners from eastern regions. The king of the country in which the rebel had taken refuge began to feel apprehensive, and handed him over to the Assyrians. Even the kings of the island of Cyprus sent tributes to Sargon.

For twelve years, the king of Chaldaea had refused to pay his tribute, and sought to foment uprisings against the Assyrians. He had formed an alliance with the king of Susiana, who had made his army available to him; however, when Sargon advanced down the Tigris and invaded Susiana, these troops returned to their own country to defend it. Sargon then turned his attention to the Chaldaeans. Babylon dared not resist; Sargon met no opposition when he entered the city, where he offered sacrifices to the gods of the city, and had himself proclaimed *king of Babylon*.

The king of Chaldaea had retired to a defensive position in the fortress of Dur-Iakina, near the sea, and had taken the precaution of flooding the plain by breaking the dikes. Fighting raged outside the city and along the canals; the Chaldaeans were eventually defeated and their

king fled, leaving behind his golden palanquin, his golden throne, his golden scepter and ornaments, together with his silver chariots, and took refuge inside the fortress of Dur-Iakina; Sargon took the citadel by storm, capturing the king, his wife, children, treasures, palace servants and all the other inhabitants. Then he set fire to the city and demolished the ramparts.

Having conquered all neighboring territories, Sargon felt a need for an entirely new capital bearing his name. Eleven miles from Nineveh, on the banks of a small river, he chose a vacant site, on which the new capital of Dur-Sharrukin (or *palace of Sargon*—the modern Khorsabad) was built. The streets of the city were laid out according to a regular plan, and the perimeter was guarded by fortified defenses.

A huge embankment covering 25 acres was built near the perimeter; its construction required 1,400,000 cubic yards of earth, all of which was moved on the backs of Sargon's captive labor force.

Sargon's palace was then built on this embankment; it had more than 200 rooms; the beams were made of cedar, cypress, ebony, and pistachio-wood. The gates were guarded by colossal creatures with the body of a bull and the head of a man. The walls were embellished with enamelled brick and alabaster bas-reliefs, depicting scenes from Sargon's campaigns, while a series of inscriptions described the details of his victories.

Sargon moved into his new capital with his whole court, his treasures and the idols of his gods in 706. He had been living in it for one year when he was assassinated.

Sennacherib and Esarhaddon

At the time of his death, his son, Sennacherib, who was then governor of Babylon, went to Assyria and had himself proclaimed king. But the tributary peoples of the Assyrians had revolted on hearing of Sargon's death, and Sennacherib had to start the whole process of conquest all over again.

His preparations for this endeavor lasted two years.

First, he struck against the king of Kar-Dunias who was occupying Chaldaea, engaging him in a major battle a few miles outside Babylon; the king of Kar-Dunias fled into the marshes, leaving behind all his equipment and animals. Sennacherib then entered Babylon and took possession of all his treasures and led away into captivity all his wives, nobles and warriors. Next he conquered 79 fortresses and 828 villages, removing their inhabitants also. As king of Babylon he appointed Belibus, the son of a Babylonian astrologer, who had been raised in his palace. On his way back to Nineveh, he looted and destroyed everything along the banks of the Euphrates, eventually returning in triumph to his capital with 2,800 prisoners, both men and women, 7,200 horses or mules, 5,330 camels, 70,000 head of cattle and 810,000 sheep.

His next campaign was in Syria, where the petty princes had refused to pay tribute, and had formed an alliance with the king of Egypt. In one swift movement Sennacherib crossed the mountains and struck deep into the territory of his adversaries. Most of the kings fled; the ruler of Ascalon, however, stood his ground and was captured, along with his wife, children, family and gods and led back to captivity in Assyria. The rulers of Lower Egypt attacked the Assyrians but were sent reeling back. The kingdom of Judah was plundered throughout and 200,000 people were deported as captives of the Assyrians. Sennacherib then entered Egypt, shortly after the king of Ethiopia had done likewise; however, he was obliged to withdraw without engaging him in battle, as the Assyrian army had been hit hard by an epidemic.

Meanwhile, there had been yet another uprising in Chaldaea. Sennacherib made a hurried return to Babylon, entering the city with no opposition. Then he invaded the Sealands; the king of Bit-Yakin fled by sea with the idols of his gods, but his family was taken prisoner, his cities destroyed and his nobles led away to captivity. The elder son of Sennacherib was made king of Chaldaea.

Those among the inhabitants of Bit-Yakin who had managed to escape had settled in Susiana, and eventually went to war again. Having arranged for Phoenician sailors to come to Nineveh, Sennacherib built a fleet of ships which took only five days to descent the Tigris and reach the sea. Sennacherib offered a sacrifice to the god of the Ocean, by tossing into the sea a number of small gold model ships and gold fish. Then he disembarked in Susiana, advanced throughout the territory, looting and destroying as he went, and then left, with his prisoners and booty, on the same ships that had taken him there.

While Sennacherib had been thus busily putting down revolts far from home, an uprising occurred in Babylon; Sennacherib returned and

Sennacherib holding an audience in his palace at Nineveh. Reconstruction based on actual fragments from the period.

captured Mushezib-Marduk, the leader of the revolt, whom he sent back to Assyria. In the following spring, he made another attack on Susiana, taking 34 fortresses, deporting the inhabitants, and installing people he had taken prisoner in the west in their place.

Mushezib-Marduk, however, had managed to escape and return to Babylon, where he was proclaimed king and assumed ownership of the treasures assembled in the main temple of the city. Having sought and received help from the king of Susiana, Mushezib-Marduk, with a vast army composed of Chaldaeans and various disaffected vassals of the Assyrians, engaged Sennacherib in a massive battle at Halule, on the Diyala. The Assyrians won. Sennacherib related the episode in his own vivid language: "All over the blood-soaked earth, a tangle of weapons and harnesses lay like wreckage on a river made of the blood of my enemies; their mangled bodies lay crushed by my war-chariots. I made a pile of their corpses, as a triumphant gesture, and cut off their hands and feet. When I caught any of the enemy alive, I cut off their hands as a punishment."

The victorious Sennacherib took a terrible revenge on Babylon, burning the city to the ground, demolishing ramparts and temples, and dumping the debris in the Euphrates canal.

On his return to Assyria, he put his prisoners to work expanding Nineveh, digging channels and building a new palace, on which the following inscription was engraved: "The supreme lord, Ashur, has made me the master of all the inhabitants of the earth. The enemy kings, filled with fear, did not dare to deploy their troops before me, they fled like a flock of birds, in order not to meet me."

Shortly afterwards, while he was in the act of offering sacrifice to his god, Sennacherib was assassinated by two of his sons (681). The Assyrians, however, refused to give their allegiance to the murderers; it was another son of the slain king, Esarhaddon, who succeeded him.

He rebuilt the Babylon which his father had destroyed. In fact, he himself, dressed in a stone-mason's clothes, laid the first brick. His life, like the lives of those who had preceded him on the throne of Assyria, was one endless succession of expeditions, against the people of the mountainous north, against the Chaldaeans, and against Syria. He even tried to cross the Arabian desert, in order to reach the prodigious treasures which were said to be amassed beyond it. After marching for several days, his army reached a desolate area, which the Assyrians named the *land of thirst;* for a few days, he found nothing but a rocky landscape inhabited by scorpions and snakes. Eventually, he called a halt when faced by steeply rising ground, and ordered his army to return the way they had come.

Esarhaddon made one more visit to Syria, this time invading Egypt, forcing the king of Ethiopia to flee, and advancing up the Nile valley. He captured Thebes and sacked the entire city, sending the statues and ornaments from the temples back to Assyria. He then installed Assyrian soldiers in the Delta fortresses; he divided Egypt among twenty petty kings who recognized his suzerainty, and paid tribute to him.

He conferred upon himself the title of "king of the kings of Egypt" (671).

On his way back, he crossed Syria, pausing for a while at Nar-el-Kelb; here, on a rock face overlooking the fast-flowing river, Ramses II of Egypt had once commemorated his victories in a series of carved inscriptions. Esarhaddon added some inscriptions of his own, describing his conquest of Egypt, and also had his own image cut into the rock. Then, he summoned all the kings of Syria to come and make submission to him; twenty-two complied with his command.

Upon his return to Assyria, he built a new palace, at Calah; leading up to its main entrance was a colossal ceremonial staircase, while three rows of winged lions and sphinxes stood guard at the portico itself. Its doors were made of ebony, with plaques of iron, ivory and silver. The carved cedar-wood roof was supported on rows of columns made of cypress-wood, plated with metal.

Ashurbanipal

Esarhaddon decided that the time had come for him to retire from the life of the battlefield; so, in 668, he withdrew to Babylon and handed over his throne to his son, Ashurbanipal.

Ashurbanipal offering libations to the gods at one of his banquets (Baghdad Museum).

A new round of wars then took place, against Egypt, Syria, Armenia and Susiana.

In Egypt, the Assyrians routed the army of the king of Ethiopia, and advanced as far as Thebes. Once they had left, however, the king of Ethiopia retook Thebes and Memphis, and those Assyrians who had stayed behind in Egypt were defeated and taken prisoner. Ashurbanipal found that he had to reconquer the whole of Egypt; this time, he sacked Thebes, removing the gold, silver, precious stones, fabrics, horses, and slaves he found there, together with two obelisks, covered with sculptures, which had stood outside one of the temples.

There was unrest in Syria, too; the Assyrians forced the insurgent Phoenician kings to surrender their daughters, who were promptly sent back to Nineveh.

But the worst carnage took place in the east, in Susiana and Chaldaea.

The king of Susiana, Teuman, was defeated, captured and then beheaded in the presence of the entire army; his head was taken back to Nineveh, where, for a long time, it was left impaled on a spear outside one of the gates of the city. Two messengers, whom Teuman had dispatched to the king of Assyria before his defeat, reached Nineveh without having learnt of the intervening events, and suddenly noticed their master's head; one of them committed suicide, while the other was put in chains. Two other chieftains from Susiana were taken to Arbela, where their tongues were cut out; they were then flayed alive and tossed into a red-hot furnace. As a deterrent to any would-be insurgents in Susiana, the Assyrians cut off the lips of Teu-

man's sons and then sent them back home in this badly mutilated state.

In Chaldaea, Ashurbanipal's younger brother, the governor of Babylon, revolted against his rule; the wealth accumulated in his temples was such that he could easily afford to equip an army. However, he never moved from Babylon; after a siege, he and his troops were reduced to desperate famine, in which they started eating the flesh of their own children. He himself was captured and burnt alive. Those of his soldiers who had not been starved to death or killed themselves in despair were treated, in Ashurbanipal's own words, in the following way: "I ripped out the tongues of those officers whose mouths had blasphemed against Ashur, my master, and then slaughtered them; any soldiers who were found still alive were flogged in front of the winged bulls built by Sennacherib, my grandfather; I whipped them on Sennacherib's tomb, and then tossed their quivering flesh for the jackals, the birds and the fish to eat. In this way I placated the wrath of the gods who had become incensed by their ignominious deeds."

More fighting broke out, this time on the initiative of the king of Susiana. The Assyrians invaded his country and ransacked his capital city, Susa. Ashurbanipal removed all the gold, silver and statues of the deities; he smashed the colossal statues of winged lions and bills, burnt the sacred wood, tore the sanctuaries apart and mutilated the statues of the kings. He then withdrew, leaving a scene of devastation behind him, and taking into captivity the enemy officers, royal family and warriors. In his own words: "The whole country was now without

villages, livestock or fields. I have left it for the wild donkeys, the gazelles and the animals of the desert to roam around at will." The storming of Susa is shown in the bas-reliefs of his palace, together with scenes in which prisoners are being flayed alive, having their eyes gouged out, their ears chopped off, and their beard and nails torn out. Ashurbanipal held a triumphal parade in Nineveh, in which he was pulled along in a chariot drawn by four captive kings.

Ashurbanipal did much to enhance the beauty of Nineveh; he repaired the palace of Sennacherib and added several new rooms. The walls were covered with bas-reliefs depicting the king at war and out hunting.

The palace library was composed of a collection of terra cotta tablets, both sides of which were covered with minute script. Piles of such tablets were discovered when the site was explored, many of them broken; they were taken to England, where they were deciphered, and shown to consist of grammars, dictionaries, lists of officers and cities, treatises on mathematics and astronomy, and, most particularly, books on magic. The tablets occupy a total volume of some 110 cubic yards, which is thought to be about the equivalent of five hundred tomes of five hundred pages each.

The destruction of Nineveh

Ashurbanipal, as we know, was the last of the powerful Assyrian kings. He was succeeded by his son, about whose reign we know nothing.

About this time, bands of horsemen swept out of the northern steppes, invaded Assyria

and Asia Minor, and spread havoc throughout the region for several years.

Then the governor of Babylon, Nabopolassar, rebelled and became king of Chaldaea. He formed an alliance with the king of the Medes, who had just established a powerful kingdom: his son married the daughter of the king of the Medes. The Chaldaeans and the Medes then attacked Assyria together. Nineveh fell. According to one account of the battle, the king of Assyria (whose name is uncertain), burned himself to death in his own palace, on seeing the enemy enter the city.

Every city in Assyria, Calah, Dur-sharrukin, Ashur, Nineveh were burnt to the ground and totally devastated; none of them were ever rebuilt. The victorious armies even diverted the river Tigris through the streets of Nineveh, so that even the place where the city had once stood should be lost forever. Within a few years, no-one was able to say for sure where the capital city of once-powerful Assyria had actually stood.

The Greeks, who were unfamiliar with the history of Assyria, had a legend about the fall of Nineveh which, through them, became quite well known.

The story was that Nineveh, at one time, had a lazy and apparently spineless king called Sardanapal, who loved to dress up in women's clothes. One day, the captain of the Royal guard, a Mede, happened to look into one of the more remote rooms in the palace, and, to his great surprise, found the king dressed as a woman, holding a distaff. Filled with revulsion at the thought of having such an incompetent fop for a monarch, he suggested to the governor of Babylon that they should start an uprising and depose him. The two of them formed an alliance with the army chiefs; a revolt ensued.

However, Sardanapal reacted to this danger by suddenly becoming vigorous and warlike. Even though he was defeated in battle, he shut himself up in Nineveh and, for two years, resisted his attackers successfully. Eventually the Tigris overflowed and caused a part of the brick ramparts to collapse, whereupon Sardanapal, seeing that all was lost, built a huge bonfire in the middle of his palace, piled up his gold, silver, and richly embroidered garments and then burnt himself alive together with his wives and slaves.

Reconstruction of Babylon.

3. The Babylonian Empire

A new Chaldaean kingdom

During the period of Assyrian rule over Chaldaea, a new nation came to be formed in the region, made up of people who were quite unlike the ancient Chaldaeans. Like the Assyrians themselves, these new Chaldaeans were warriors, who, in the words of one of the Jewish prophets, "used to strike with incredible speed and cruelty, plundering mercilessly as they swept through the lands of their helpless victims . . . Their horses were lighter on their feet than the leopard and swifter than the wolves who hunt at nightfall."

While governor of Babylon, Nabopolassar rebelled against the king of Assyria and was proclaimed king of Chaldaea.

After the destruction of Nineveh, he became the ruler of Mesopotamia and of the whole of the Euprates basin. The petty kings of Phoenicia and Syria, whom he regarded as his vassals, were required to pay to him the tribute which they had formerly paid to the king of Assyria; just to make sure that they did, he sent his son with an army to assert his rule over them.

He repaired the dikes and canals of the Euphrates, and did much to rebuild the inner city of Babylon itself, as well as the other cities of Chaldaea, as the whole area had suffered immense devastation during the reign of Ashurbanipal. He began to restore the ramparts of the city of Babylon and to rebuild the palace. Yet he was already quite an old man when he set about these tasks, and died before he could finish them (604).

Nebuchadnezzar

His son, Nebuchadnezzar, who bore the title of king even before his father's death, was one of the most famous monarchs of antiquity. He fought several wars, all of them in the West.

Emboldened by the destruction of the Assyrian empire, the king of Egypt, Necho, had invades Syria and compelled the petty Syrian kings to declare themselves his vassals. Nebuchadnezzar set out to stop him. The two armies met in a huge battle on the banks of the Euphrates, at Carchemish, where the Egyptians were routed, and bolted in disorder for Egypt. Nebuchadnezzar reconquered the whole of Syria and was able to pursue the retreating Egyptians as far as their own borders (604). However, on hearing of the death of his father, he returned to Babylon.

The king of Egypt's ambitions towards Syria had not been abandoned; he stirred up unrest among the petty kings of Palestine and Phoenicia, with the result that they, together with the king of Judah, rebelled against the Chaldaeans. Nebuchadnezzar returned and subdued the Jews (597).

A few years later, the new king of Egypt, Hophra (Apries), went to war in Syria; whereupon the Jews and the Syrians seized the opportunity and rebelled. Nebuchadnezzar returned in force to Syria, determined to settle matters there once and for all. After a siege, he took Jerusalem, destroyed it and deported its inhabitants to Babylon. He then surrounded Tyre, in a siege which is thought by some to have lasted thirteen years; he failed to take the city, but did ruin its trade and compelled the

king to declare himself his vassal. It was expected that he would also try to conquer Egypt, but he only made a small expedition into the country.

Nebuchadnezzar says nothing about his wars in any of his inscriptions; yet he was renowned throughout Asia as a great conqueror. At a later date, the Greeks claimed that he had crossed the whole of Europe with his armies, and reached the *Pillars of Hercules* (the Straits of Gibraltar).

In the eyes of the Jews, whom he had ruined and taken away into captivity, he was the most powerful king the world had ever known. But they spoke of him with deep-seated hatred as a whimsical tyrant.

As the Bible relates, one day, Nebuchadnezzar had a dream, in which he saw a colossal statue: its head was made of gold, its arms and chest were of silver, its belly and thighs were of bronze, its legs of steel, but it had clay feet. As he stood there admiring it, a stone became dislodged from the hillside, rolled down and hit the statue's clay foot; the statue promptly collapsed, and even its wreckage disappeared. The stone which had caused such destruction became a huge mountain which filled the whole earth. Nebuchadnezzar consulted the Chaldaean soothsayers, but they were unable to explain his dream. Eventually, the Jewish prophet Daniel explained it.

According to the Bible, Nebuchadnezzar, as

Left: Jewish women (Louvre). Right: king offering tribute (Baghdad Museum).

a punishment for his pride, was made to go mad. As he looked out admiringly over his capital one day, from the terrace of his palace, he heard a heavenly voice saying: "Listen to me, Nebuchadnezzar; your kingdom is going to pass into other hands. You shall be expelled from the society of men; you shall live among the animals of the fields until you recognize that the Eternal One has absolute power over the kingdoms of the earth, and grants them to whomsoever he chooses."

Nebuchadnezzar went mad and thought he had been turned into a bull. He ran from the royal palace and went crawling, on all fours, through the fields, bellowing and eating grass. After a while he became revoltingly dirty, with hair like an eagle's feathers and nails like the claws of a bird of prey. Seven months later he was cured and recognized the power of the God of the Jews.

The greatest city in the world

Nebuchadnezzar devoted most of his energies to fortifying the cities of Chaldaea and further enhancing their beauty. He made Babylon the greatest city in the world, the "queen of Asia". Herodotus, who saw it one and a half centuries later, declared that there was no other city which could be compared with it.

Babylon was built on the plain, on either side of the Euphrates, and had two surrounding walls. The outer wall, which went round the whole city, made a square, with each side measuring about nine miles; the area thus enclosed was about the size of New York City. A wide,

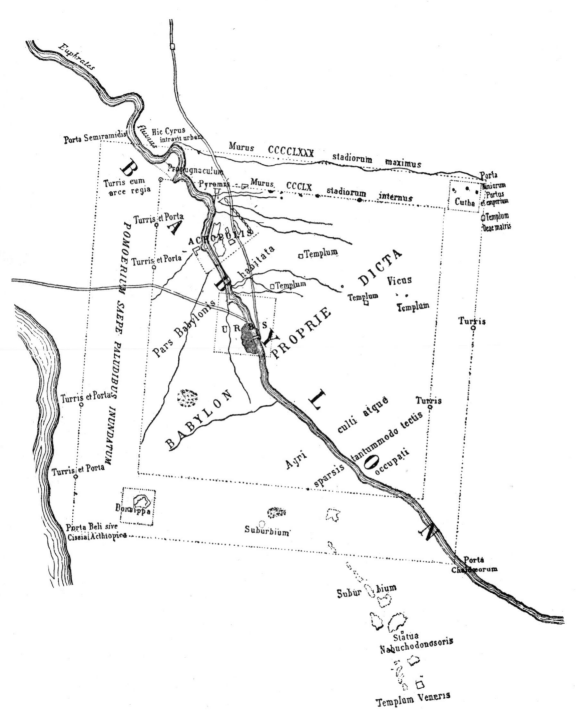

Euphrates

Porta Semiramidis

Hic Cyrus
intravit urbem

Murus CCCCLXXX stadiorum maximus

Porta
Ninorum
Portus
et emporium

Propugnaculum

Murus CCCLX stadiorum internus

Cutha

Turris eum
arce regia

Pyramis

Templum
Deae matris

B

A

Turris et Porta

ACROPOLIS

Templum

DICTA

Vicus

POMOERIUM SAEPE PALUDIBUS INUNDATUM

Turris et Porta

habitata

Templum

Templum

Templum

B

Y

L

Templum

Pars Babylonis

URBS

PROPRIE

Turris

Turris et Portas

Turris

O

Ayri

culti atque

Turris et Porta

BABYLON

sparsis tantummodo tectis

occupati

Borsippa

Porta Beli sive
Cissia Aethiopica

Suburbium

Porta
Chaldaeorum

Subur bium

Statua
Nabuchodonosoris

Templum Veneris

Views of Babylon. Right: the Lion of Babylon. Following pages: remains of a paved street in Babylon, leading to the palace of Nebuchadnezzar. One of the city gates (reconstruction).

Ruins of Babylon, with the walls of the palace of Semiramis.
Above: frieze of the gate of Babylon (reconstruction).

Upper left: aerial view of the excavations at Babylon; below: Southern Palace, reconstructed from fragments. Above: view of the ruins.

Almost all the splendor of Babylon—a city about the size of 19th century London, by all accounts—were concentrated in that part of it known as the "royal city", most of which was on the left bank of the Euphrates. This eastern section was triangular in shape; a smaller section was to be found on the other bank of the river, which ran for 2 miles through the city.

The superb residence of Nebuchadnezzar is now a shapeless ruin, known as the Ksar or Mudgelibeh, still covering 28 acres. The most famous temples were those of *Sin* (the Moon), *Shamash* (the Sun), *Bin,* the god of meteorological phenomena, *Marduk,* the patron of Babylon, *Anunit,* the celestial Venus, and *Mylitta,* the goddess of physical love.

The famous Hanging Gardens, one of the wonders of the world, are now the hill of Amran-ibn-Ali, a mound covering an area of about 32 acres. This huge mass of ruins is separated from the Ksar by a deep valley. At one time, the Euphrates used to flow past the foot of this hill. According to the Jewish historian Josephus, Nebuchadnezzar had these gardens built, in the form of an artifical mountain, as a way of consoling one of his wives, a Mede by birth, who was homesick for the mountains of her native land. There were promenades built under the vaults which supported embankments of rich earth planted with a great variety of trees. According to Strabo, the huge pillars which supported these vaults were hollow inside and were filled with earth, so as to accommodate the roots of the tallest trees. They were built of kiln-fired clay bricks, bound together with asphalt. Stairways provided access from one level to the next, and pumps raised water from the river to irrigate the plants in the gardens.

The walls which formed the outer fortifications of Babylon were made of bricks, joined together with mortar made from asphalt. These walls had 250 towers and were protected by a broad moat which had been filled with water from the Euphrates. A hundred bronze doors, with bronze frames and thresholds led into the city itself. A boulevard 65 yards wide ran the whole length of the outer wall. The city contained fifty streets (25 parallel to the Euphrates, and 25 at right angles to it) leading to a hundred bronze gates, and dividing the city into a great number of squares, only a small number of which were actually built on, as we have seen.

Between the two parts of the city flowed the Euphates, over which there was only one bridge.

Babylon: bas-reliefs of molded bricks.

79

deep moat, always full of water, ran the whole length of the outer wall. The earth removed during the digging of the moat had been used to bake bricks, which were then used to build the wall. They were cemented together with bitumen, of which plentiful deposits exist in Chaldaea. The bricks were arranged in layers, and reed-mats were inserted every thirty rows to strengthen the wall.

This outer wall was 300 feet high and 80 feet thick; the top was so wide that two chariots could drive abreast along it. It had 250 towers, arranged in pairs, and a hundred doors made of solid bronze.

High embankments made of bricks had been built along both banks of the Euphrates where it flows through the city, and there were ramps leading to them from the gates that opened on to the river. The two banks were joined by a stone bridge, the upper part of which was made of square cedarwood beams which were removed at nightfall and repaced in the morning. According to Herodotus, the bridge was cut in this way so as to prevent people crossing over in the night to commit burglaries on the other side.

The houses in Babylon were two or three stories high, arranged on a grid-pattern which divided the city into equal squares. There were 25 streets running parallel to the Euphrates, and 25 at right angles to it, each of them leading on either side to one of the hundred gates in the outer wall.

Streets accounted for only a small part of the huge area enclosed by the outer defenses, most of it being covered with gardens and fields of wheat. This was no more city, it was a whole area which had been transformed into an enclosed camp, almost big enough to feed all its inhabitants.

The monuments of Babylon

On the left bank of the Euphrates, in the middle of the enclosure, Nebuchadnezzar rebuilt the royal city. He himself gives an account of this undertaking in an inscription: "As soon as the god Marduk had summoned me to be king, I promptly and vigorously set about the reconstruction of the city. In Babylon, which I love like the apple of my eye, I built a palace which was the admiration of all those who saw it, and which I made the seat of my government. It stood on a high embankment, which stretched from the banks of the Euphrates for a long way inland. My father, Nabopolassar, had built this palace of bricks and had lived in it for some time, but a flood caused the foundations to collapse. Once the debris had been cleared away, down to the waterlevel, I built a huge dike, of bricks and bitumen, as tall as a mountain. In my palace, I built rooms with thick cedar beams, with doors made of cedar and bronze." This immense palace, the ruins of which cover about 35 acres, was joined to a large, well-fortified castle, on the side nearest the center of the city, complete with turrets and alabaster battlements.

Near the palace, along the banks of the river, were situated the famous *Hanging Gardens of Babylon,* which were later counted among the *Seven Wonders of the World.* These Gardens consisted of a series of terraces, supported by

"Reconstruction" of the Tower of Babel; this 17th-century engraving, a work of pure imagination, is included for its curiosity value.

huge vaults, which rose in stages from the river's edge and which contained a luxuriant growth of rare trees and plants. In order to maintain the health of all these exotic plants in the blazing sun of the Chaldaean plain, a powerful pump had been built inside the terrace wall, and kept up a steady flow of river water which ensured that the soil was always moist. A story was told later about the building of the Hanging Gardens. It was that a certain king of Babylon had a wife who had been born in Media, and who never succeeded in getting used to the treeless Chaldaean plain. So the king had these gardens built specially to remind her of the forests and mountains of her native land.

Under Nebuchadnezzar, every temple in Babylon was rebuilt. He himself lists eight which were built within the city itself. The biggest one was that dedicated to the god Marduk, the Esagila. The tallest cedars from the mountains of Lebanon were used in the building of this temple; the beams were decorated with gold and silver.

Near Babylon, there two cities which were famous for their sanctuaries: Cuthah, in the north, and Borsippa, in the south; both were now inside the new outer wall. Nebuchadnezzar finished the temple to the god Nergal, at Cuthah; while, at Borsippa, he had three temples built to the goddess Nana. An act particularly worthy of note was the rebuilding of the famous temple of Bel, the E-Zida, known as the *Tower of Babel*. This enormous, seven-story tower stood on an embankment 75 feet high; the sanctuary of the deity, on the top floor, had doors inlaid with ivory and beams lined with

Battle scenes figure prominently in the work of Assyrian artists. Amongst other things, we learn much about the pitiful fate of the vanquished. Assyrian vengeance was cruel and implacable. The pathetic losers can be seen prostrating themselves in the dust, kissing the king's knees; convoys of prisoners are herded around, their hands and feet in irons; they are tortured, flayed alive and their skin is stretched out on the ramparts. Others die in agony, impaled on spikes. Further on in the same scene, one may see the Assyrians counting the heads of the defeated enemy, heads which will be heaped up in bloody pyramids outside the city gates.

Those whose lives have been spared set off sadly for a distant country; they walk along naked, unarmed, their wives and children almost naked also, carrying a few scant possessions. This was the kind of mass deportation of which the Jews of Samaria are only a fairly common example. Meanwhile, the victorious soldiers parade past the king, in a brilliant military display, to the sound of triumphant music; they carry with them the trophies of war — enemy chariots, the throne of the enemy king, precious goblets, and, on their shoulders, the statues of the enemy gods; this procession is followed by more mundane sort of booty — herds of cattle, sheep and goats.

An Assyrian ship. Right: paving stones, Babylon.

gold. Nebuchadnezzar had this to say about it: "In order to astound all who might behold it, I rebuilt the marvellous temple of Borsippa, the temple of the seven spheres of the world . . . I have neither changed its position nor altered its foundations . . . I have rebuilt it just the way it must have in ancient times, slightly raising its upper part."

Nebuchadnezzar also rebuilt the temples in other towns of Chaldaea, taking great pride in his architectural achievements. "I am the great restorer and builder of holy places, the king and high priest who has enhanced the beauty of all the holy cities," these being his own words, found on an inscription. Even today, among the ruins of Babylon, millions of bricks are to be found, each bearing the following words: "I am Nebuchadnezzar, king of Babylon, rebuilder of Esagila and E-Zida, elder son of Nabopolassar."

Trade in Babylon

Nebuchadnezzar also repaired the old royal canal, built 2,000 years earlier by Hammurabi, which had silted up and become blocked. He dug new irrigation canals, and a number of canals for navigation between the Tigris and the Euphrates. Upstream from Babylon, a huge lake, with a perimeter of 40 miles, was hollowed out of the ground, to act as a catchment for the floodwaters from the Euphrates, which served as a vast reservoir for use in time of drought.

Prisoners brought back by Nebuchadnezzar from his expeditions were settled within the new defensive wall; the population grew, and Babylon became the greatest trading center of Asia.

Ships used to come from India and Arabia, across the Persian Gulf and up the Euphrates, bringing cargoes of fabrics, perfumes, spices, ivory, ebony and precious stones.

Trade reaching Babylon from the Armenian mountains followed an interesting pattern: small, round boats, shaped like shields, were made by stretching animal hides across a frame of willow branches; the bottom of the craft was then lined with straw and the merchandise was loaded on board. Each boat carried two men, who did the steering, and at least one donkey. Freight thus moved down the Tigris or the Euphrates as far as Babylon, where it was unloaded; the boat was then dismantled, the wooden frame sold and the hides loaded on to the donkeys for the return journey overland to the mountains.

Nitocris

By the time Herodotus visited Babylon, Nebuchadnezzar's name was hardly mentioned any more; his accomplishments were ascribed to two queens: Semiramis and Nitocris.

Herodotus was told, for example, that Nitocris had decreed that she should be buried inside one of the embankments overlooking one of the gates of the city and that the following inscription should be placed over her tomb: "If any of the kings who succeed me in Babylon ever needs money, he should open this tomb and take as much as he needs; but he should take care not to open it if his need is not great

19th-century painting showing the destruction of Babylon. Here again, the artist has drawn on authentic material from the period.

or for any reason other than money."

The tomb remained sealed until the Persian conquest. However, Darius, once he had become the ruler of Babylon, decided that it was a shame to leave all that money just sitting there, and ordered the tomb opened. All that he found inside was the body of the queen, and this inscription: "If you had not been so greedy for money, you would not have opened the tomb of the dead."

The destruction of Babylon

The successors of Nebuchadnezzar were not a very distinguished lot. The fourth of them, Nabu-na'id, who was not from the same family as Nebuchadnezzar, rebuilt a number of ancient temples in the cities of Chaldaea, and revived the cult of the deities of those cities. In fact, he himself settled in a small town outside Babylon, thus alienating the priests of the god Marduk, whose sanctuary was in Babylon.

After the conquest of Media and Lydia, Cyrus, king of the Persians, invaded Chaldaea. Nabu-na'id was defeated and taken prisoner, and the Persians met no opposition as they entered Babylon.

The Bible gives an interesting account of the fall of Babylon. The king at the time was called Balthazar. Confident that his city was impregnable, he spent his time enjoying himself in his palace with his wives and courtiers. One day, during a banquet attended by a thousand people, Balthazar, in an expansive mood after drinking plenty of strong wine, ordered his servants to bring out the gold and silver goblets which had been looted from the temple of Je-

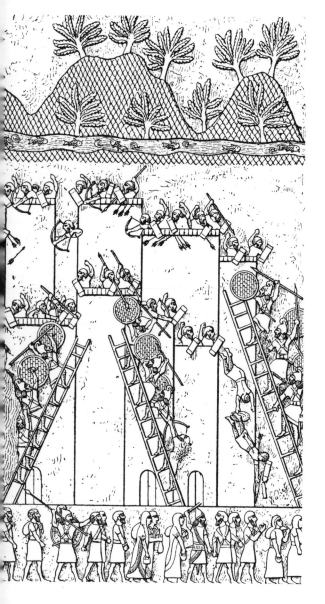

rusalem, and then drank out of them, together with all his courtiers.

At this moment, the startled guests saw a hand appear, from nowhere, and start writing on the wall of the banqueting-hall. When the king saw the fingers of the hand move, the blood drained from his face, and his knees crumpled under him. He let out a loud scream, and then summoned the Chaldaean magicians and soothsayers and said to them: "Anyone who can decipher and explain the writing on the wall will be given a purple cloak and a golden necklace and will become the third highest person in the kingdom." But no-one could read what was written on the wall.

So they sent for the Jewish prophet Daniel, who said: "This is what is written on the wall—*Mane, Thecel, Phares; Mane,* God has weighed your royalty in the balance and is putting an end to it.—*Thecel,* you have been weighed in the balance and have been found to be too light.—*Phares,* your kingdom has been divided up and given to the Medes and the Persians."

That same night, the Persians entered Babylon and Balthazar was killed.

Unlike Nineveh, Babylon was not destroyed; it continued to be the biggest city in Asia, but ceased to be the capital of an empire. The Persian kings had their seat of government in their own country, leaving only a governor in charge of Babylon.

Detail from a bas-relief: the storming of a citadel.
Right: other scenes from the ruins of Babylon. The end of an era . . .

Carved disk: a Babylonian marble. (Berlin, Staatliche Museen). – Right: detail from a bas-relief.

Left: these two arms on a bas-relief make a striking decorative theme. Right: artist's impression of a banquet given by a Babylonian dignitary.

Early votive tablet (Baghdad Museum).

4. Daily life. Religion. Science. Customs

Daily life

The Chaldaeans were a people of farmers. They plowed the soil with small carts drawn by oxen, and irrigated it with water taken from rivers or canals in buckets attached by a rope to a revolving cross-beam. They bred herds of cattle and sheep.

Fields belonging to different landlords were measured from markers fixed in the ground and were separated accordingly. Plots of such land were bought and sold.

The Chaldaens and the Assyrians were almost all town-dwellers. Their houses were most often covered with earth; in these squat structures, with their dark interiors, the people sought relief from the hot sun. The great cities abounded with craftsmen. Chaldaea used to produce beautiful woollen or linen fabrics which were then used to make clothes or carpets; these brilliantly colored fabrics, decorated with embroideries of men, animals or plants, were famous throughout the whole of antiquity. Magnificent damascene weapons, furniture made of ivory and wood inlaid with gold and silver, and superb leather saddles and harnesses were all made in Assyria and Chaldaea.

Rich citizens wore necklaces, bracelets and earrings, a linen and a woolen tunic and an embroidered cloak. They wore their hair long, in carefully curled tresses reaching right down to the shoulder, and their long wavy beards came as far their chest. Commoners wore only one tunic and went about barefoot.

The king and his lords had a number of wives, whom they kept locked up in chambers into which no-one was allowed, and which they could not leave. Common women, however, lived much freer lives, and could even go out into the street with their face uncovered.

Gods and their cult

In the earliest times, the main cities in Chaldaea and Assyria each had their own god, which the inhabitants worshipped as their master and their protector. Later, all the gods came to be worshipped simultaneously in all the cities.

The principal gods were about twelve in number.

Marduk, the god of Babylon, also known as Bel-Marduk, was the god of the sun and the prince of the legions of stars. He is depicted either as a warrior armed with a spear, bow, shield and club with which to fight off the evil spirits, or as a king seated on a throne, wearing on his head a tiara, out of which a pair of bull's horns could be seen protruding, as a sign of strength.

Ashur, the god of the Assyrians, was also shown as having the face of a warrior or a king. Often, he appears to be soaring through the sky, with a bow in one hand, in the middle of a circle borne along by two large wings.

Hea, the fish-god, is depicted as having the body of a fish and the head of a man, or a man's body covered with fish scales and the tail of an eagle. He was said to have come out of the sea to teach men the sciences and the arts, building and agriculture.

Sin, the god of Ur, was a moon-god; Sha-

The institutions the Babylonians had do not seem to have been very harsh.

The free population was divided into castes of two broad categories, *generic* castes and *craft* castes. The first of these were tribes named after a man who was thought to have been their ancestor. We know of more than a hundred such chiefs, called *banu,* or father, for example, those of Nur-Sin, Irani, Edir, Nabunnaï, Sin-emitti and, above all, Egibi, one branch of which provided the kings of Babylon with finance ministers for several centuries.

The *craft* castes were divided into two distinct categories; one very elevated category was that of the priests of the different divinities, of Ea, Bel, Ishtar, Ninib and others, of scholars, astrologers, *sapiri,* jurists. The *king's judges* do not seem to have been chosen from any single caste. They administered civil and criminal justice, ordinary cases being handled by *municipal courts,* which were presided over by a *sangu* or a *tupsav,* a public scribe or actuary. Surveyors *(masihani)* also seem to have belonged to this first class.

Very early female effigies.

The other class consisted of the craftsmen properly so called: sailors, weavers, blacksmiths, farmers and others. According to Herodotus, fishermen formed a class apart: they fed on fish, which they ground into a bread-like meal.

Herodotus also gives the impression that doctors, as such, did not exist in Babylon: the sick were simply laid out in the street, and passers-by were expected to offer advice; the choice of therapy was decided by popular consensus.

Weddings took place once a year, in a public ceremony at which girls of suitable age were put up for auction. Beautiful girls fetched a high price, and this money then went to provide dowries for the less beautiful.

Babylon's reputation for immorality derives from the religious custom which made it compulsory for every woman to give herself, once in her life, to a stranger whom she was to meet by waiting in the sanctuary of Mylitta; she did not have the right to refuse her stranger, who, in turn, had to pay a certain amount into the coffers of the temple. Apart from this purely religious custom, prostitution flourished in Babylon, as was clear from the testimony of others, besides the Jewish prophets. Herodotus said that poverty had had a demoralizing influence, and that people used to sell their own daughters into prostitution.

mash, the god of Sippar, was a sun-god who appears seated on a throne, holding the sun, in the form of an orb, in one hand, and a scepter in the other.

Ninib is represented as a powerful hunter, strangling a lion with his bare hands; his titles included those of "lord of strength", and "lord of swords and armies".

Nergal, the god of Cuthah, was a lion-god, often shown with the body of a lion and the bust of a man, or with the head of a lion on a man's body.

Raman, the god of the sky, thunder and rain, known also as the "lord of the canals, the god of fertility, and the lord of storms", appears as a warrior armed with an axe, wearing a crown with four horns on his head; in his hand he held a thunderbolt.

Nebo (the Biblical form of Nabu), the god of writing, science and divination, was depicted as an old man with a long beard, clad in a long cloak, and wearing a crown of bulls' horns. He was thought to control the movements of the stars and to be a special protector of kings.

The goddess Ishtar, who was worshipped in Arbela and Nineveh, took a variety of forms. Sometimes, she was the "queen of battles", in cuirass and helmet; or the "goddess of love", in which case she was seen holding a dove; she also took the form of a mother holding a child in her arms. An assortment of other gods were also worshipped, including Belit, Zer-banitum (Sarpanitum) and Mylitta, who might well have been the same god, only under different names.

Other, less powerful gods were thought to exist at a lower level than these major deities:
these was a god in the form of a serpent with a man's head, another one which looked like a huge bird, "the bird of storms", a harvest-god, and a god of the Euphrates.

It was thought that the major gods had genies working as servants for them; they had the body of a man, with four huge, outspread wings, or the body of gigantic winged bull, with a man's head and a lion's tail. The Assyrian kings used to have such genies standing guard outside their palace gates.

The gods themselves took the form of statues of stone, gold or silver, clad in richly embroidered fabrics. They were jealously guarded deep inside sanctuaries to which only the priests had access. On feast-days, they were brought out and carried through the streets in processions.

The cult of the gods involved animal sacrifice, the burning of incense, the pouring of libations, the chanting of prayers and the singing of hymns. The following is a prayer which Nebuchadnezzar had engraved on his statue: "Oh Marduk, lord of all countries, heed my words. I have built a temple for you; grant that I may be able to be proud of its glory. Grant that I may reach old age here in Babylon, and that my posterity may be numerous; that the kings of all the countries of the world may pay me tribute; grant that my descendants may rule over men until the end of time."

Black stone statuette, found at Mari (Aleppo Museum).

The cult of the stars

In the clear night air of Chaldaea, the stars shine with a brilliance not seen in our misty northern latitudes. Their observations of these spectacular constellations told the Chaldaeans that some of the heavenly bodies were constantly changing position: they had learnt to distinguish the planets from the stars.

They regarded the five planets, Mercury, Venus, Mars, Jupiter and Saturn, together with the Sun and the Moon, as special manifestations of the gods; they called them the *interpreters* of the gods. Each planet represented a deity and bore its name; the same color was associated with both the star and the god. Mercury (the star of Nebo) was blue; Venus (Ishtar), white; Mars (Nergal), vermilion; Jupiter (Marduk), purple; Saturn (Ninib), black; the Moon (Sin), silver; and the Sun (Shamash), gold.

The Chaldaeans had also noticed that the precise point among the constellations at which the sun rises changes as the year proceeds, and that it moves around the whole of the heavens in the course of one year; they had recognized the twelve constellations in the midst of which the sun rises successively. They also regarded these constellations as divine beings, the "lords of the gods".

Astrology and astronomy

The Chaldaeans thought that the stars were a manifestation of the will of the gods, and that, by studying their movements, it was possible to foretell events on earth.

99

The priests were therefore also divines, whose job was to foretell the coming of wind, rain, floods, heatwaves, good and bad harvests. They also foretold political events, the death of kings, wars, defeats.

But the one thing which made the Chaldaean divines famous throughout the ancient world was the art of foretelling what would happen to each individual. The Chaldaeans held that the position of the stars at the moment of a child's birth made it possible to foresee the whole of his destiny. Everyone has their own *star,* under the influence of which they remain for the rest of their lives; if it is a good star, the person will be happy; and if it is a bad star, he will be unhappy. All that one needed to know, in order to predict a man's destiny, was the star under which he had been born; this was it what the Greeks called the *horoscope.*

Looking up at the brilliant night sky over the Chaldaean plains, these people had made discoveries which later research was to prove correct. They had succeeded in calculating the movements of the planets, and forecasting eclipses of the moon. They had fixed the twelve signs of the Zodiac, established that the year consisted of 365¼ days, and invented the sundial. They were truly the creators of astronomy.

High fashion from Assyria (2,000 B.C.). Embroidery of a robe belonging to King Sennacherib, after a bas-relief from Nineveh.

100

Dress

Herodotus, who visited Babylon in the V century BC, has given us much valuable information which he had personally confirmed by his own observation, and certain other information which, though he could not vouch for its authenticity, has been of assistance to us in our study of this civilization.

Here is what he has to say about the dress of the Chaldaeans.

"They wear a linen tunic down to the feet, and, over it, a woollen tunic. They then wrap themselves in a small white cloak. Their footwear is rather like that worn by the Boeotians. They let their hair grow long, wear what looks like a mitre on their heads, and rub perfumes all over their bodies. Everyone has a seal and a hand-carved walking-stick, the top of which is in the shape of an apple, a rose, a lily or an eagle, or some other figure, as they are not permitted to carry a cane with or a stick without some characteristic ornament on it . . ."

These observations have been confirmed by modern discoveries. Statuettes have been found which correspond to this description; the cane which, as Herodotus said, was so dear to the inhabitants of Babylon, and their seal, have been found lying by the side of the bodies in Chaldaean graves.

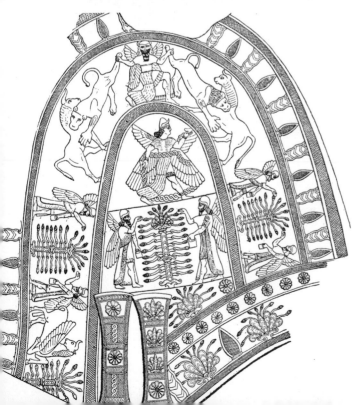

101

Ornamental work on two altars to Ashur (Berlin, Staatliche Museen and Istanbul Museum).

Right: fragment of a statue showing a deity holding a vase. (Very early work).

Demons and witchcraft

The Chaldaeans imagined that the world was full of invisible spirits, who were constantly busy causing harm to men. These evil spirits, or "spirits of darkness", as they were called, were to be found everywhere—in the air, under water and in the bowels of the earth. They were particularly abundant in the desert, whence they emerged at night in order to torment men.

In the minds of the Chaldaeans, these spirits took a variety of forms; some were ghosts, the souls of the dead, who had returned to earth to frighten the living; they even believed in the vampire, who leaves his tomb in order to devour the unwary.

The others were *demons,* depicted in sculptures as the most weird and fantastic faces; some of them had a lion's head, a man's body and the claws of an eagle. Others had the head of a hyena, the body of a bear and the paws of a lion. In the Louvre, there is a bronze statuette of a standing demon, which has a pair of goat's horns protruding from the head of a dead man, the body of a dog, the feet of an eagle, the tail of a scorpion, a pair of man's arms ending in lion's claws, and huge outstretched wings. This is the demon of the south-east wind, which comes off the hot desert sands, drying the moisture out of everything in its path.

The Chaldaeans believed that all accidents and, most particularly, all diseases, were the work of demons; there was a demon of the plague, a demon of the fever, and a demon of ulcers. Whenever anyone fell ill, it was assumed that a demon had got into his body; this was also

the standard explanation for fits of madness, of epilepsy, and also for nervous breakdowns.

Cure took the form of trying to expel the demon from the patient's body. The Chaldaeans had a number of procedures for doing this, which they devised at a very early stage in their history, and which they used for thousands of years.

One method was to invoke a powerful god who might come and help fight the demon: for example, the god Marduk, or the god of fire. His assistance was implored with the following words: "Fire, destroyer of enemies, terrible weapon which destroys the plague, brilliant, fertile fire, destroy this evil".

Another method involved placing the image of a god or a benign genie outside the house, in order to scare away the demons. The colossal winged bulls with men's heads who stood guard on either side of the entrance to Sargon's palace were intended as a deterrent against evil spirits. Statues of Bel, Nergal and Nebo have been found been the threshold of this same palace. Other images were also used, for example, that of a god, in the form of a lion or a bull, in the act of crushing evil spirits to death.

It was also thought that demons could be chased away by other demons, or even that they would take fright at the sight of their own image. This accounts for the presence in Chaldaean houses of statues or bas-reliefs of the most horrid-looking demons. The palace of Ashurbanipal was found to contain demons with the head of a lion and the feet of an eagle, each armed with a dagger and locked in a mortal struggle with each other.

The commonest methods involved the use of magic incantations and amulets. Certain words

and gestures were assumed to have particular power which the demons were unable to withstand.

In order to cure the sick person, a special form of words was recited over him, commanding the evil spirits to go away. For example: "Let the evil demon leave; let the demons strike at each other. May the good spirit enter his body". Another example: "The plague and fever which are laying waste the whole country, the evil demon, the wicked man, the evil eye, the slanderous mouth and tongue—may they all come out from this body, and from its entrails. They shall never enter into my body, they shall never do any evil before me, they shall never enter into my house.—Spirit of the heavens, remember this! Spirit of the earth, remember this!"

Another belief of theirs was that certain plants had the power to chase out demons. The sick were given infusions of the leaves of these plants to drink.

Magic knots were also used, as in the following remedy for a certain kind of headache: "Arrange a woman's diadem so that it is knotted on the right side and lies in flat bands on the left; divide it twice into seven strips; put it around the patient's head, forehead, feet and hands; sit him down on his bed and pour magic waters over him. May his sickness be swept away into the skies, like the strong wind, may it be buried like the waters under the earth."

Alabaster statuette from Babylon (about 300 B.C.). Right: a curious subject for a bas-relief – a genie offering poppies (about 800 B.C.)

The amulets used were either strips of fabric on which a magic formula had been written, or precious stones or necklaces bearing the image of a divinity, or some special form of words, such as the following: "Evil demon, malignant Plague, the Spirit of the Earth has driven you out of his body. May the favorable genie, the good giant, the benign spirit, come with the Spirit of the Earth. Incantation of the powerful, powerful, powerful god."

People used to wear these amulets around their neck or on their clothes; they were also kept inside the rooms of a house or inserted into the foundations in order to drive away the demons.

The Chaldaeans believed that there were special incantations which could make demons come, just as there were others to make them go away. Demons could be made to work both ways, they believed: they could be expelled from the body of a sick man, thus making him healthy again, and they could also be summoned into the body of a healthy man, thus making him sick. Accordingly, everyone lived in mortal dread of the wizards, who were called the "evildoers". They were thought to be able to destroy crops, make hail fall and transmit diseases, either by uttering certain magic words, or by giving people magic potions to drink, or by looking at their victims in a certain way.

Throughout the whole of antiquity, the Chaldaeans remained famous as divines, magicians and wizards. The belief in the power of magic spells, potions, the evil eye, lucky charms, talismans and amulets which all civilized peoples have adopted, and which still survives throughout the Middle and Far East (and even

"The tree of life": an ancient and very central theme, here portrayed on a bas-relief from the palace of Ashur-nasir-pal.
Right: this vase is a remarkable specimen of ceramic art from the classical period (Louvre).

*Scenes from daily life . . . The harpist on the left be-
longs to the period when Babylon was at its the
height of its power. (Baghdad Museum).*

in the West, among less well educated segments of the population), can be traced back to them. As late as the Middle Ages, in Europe, there were incantations still in use which actually used Assyrian words; for example: "Hilka, hilka, bescha, bescha". (Go away, go away, bad, bad.).

Weights and measures

The Chaldaeans invented all the methods for the measurement of time, length, and weight used by the other peoples of antiquity.

They divided the year into twelve months, some of 29 days and the others of 30 days, in accordance with the rotation of moon. This made their year shorter than the true year of 365 1/4 days, calculated from the rotation of the earth around the sun. To make up the difference, they inserted a thirteenth month, of 30 days, once every six years. They were the ones who devised the seven-day week, in honor of the seven planets; the seventh day was a day of rest, on which no-one should fight, nor administer justice, nor even take medication. They were the ones who divided the day into 24 hours, the hour into 60 minutes and the minute into 60 seconds.

They also were responsible for the division of the circle into 360 degrees, of the degree into 60 minutes, the minute into 60 seconds, and the second into 60 thirds, for which they used the signs ° for degree, ' for minute, " for second, and ''' for tierce.

They also devised a complete system of measurements.

Units of length were the span (11 inches), the cubit (1 ft. 8 ins.), the perch, which consisted of 12 spans, the plethra (10 perches) and the stadium.

Units of surface measurement were the square foot, the square cubit and the square stadium.

The units of weight were the mine (1 lb. 2 oz) and the talent (60 mines). The mine was divided into 60 drachmas.

Geometrical problem, on a cuneiform tablet. Babylon, about 1,600 B.C. (Baghdad Museum).

5. Architecture. Script

Architecture

The Chaldaeans and the Assyrians built a great number of monuments, the ruins of which now lie scattered across the landscape in huge mounds.

The architects of Chaldaea had no stone for building purposes; they made bricks out of moistened, kneaded clay which they cast in molds. The *baked* bricks, which were made in ovens, became red and very hard. *Unbaked* bricks were simply dried in the sun; they retained a whitish coloring, and were much more brittle than the first kind of brick, being used for embankments and thick outer walls.

Bricks were usually a foot long and four inches thick, and bore an inscription made with a metal stamp while the clay was still wet. The bricks were held together by lime or clay mortar, and quite often by bitumen. Buildings made with such bricks had to have enormously thick walls which could never be very tall and could not have windows.

Even though stone was obtainable from the mountains of Assyria, the Assyrian architects kept the same system, using stone only for the foundations, floors and bas-reliefs.

Thousands of men were required to knead and mold these enormous masses of clay, and to move and lay the millions of bricks and the huge sculptures which covered them. It was all done by the forced labor of prisoners of war brought back by the kings from their campaigns, under the supervision of club-wielding guards.

The first act in the building process was a religious ceremony. The king would come in person and deposit in the foundations a cylinder of stone and clay (the *temen*), which bore a commemorative inscription. It was also customary to deposit statuettes, amulets and plaques of gold, silver and copper.

An Assyrian palace

Remnants of the palaces of seven or eight Assyrian kings have been found, the most famous of them,—and the best preserved—being the palace of king Sargon, at Khorsabad.

This palace was built on a huge square embankment, covering 24 acres and so arranged that each corner pointed exactly to the four points of the compass. Those approaching it on foot had to climb enormous expanses of stairs, while vehicles went up a long, gently sloping ramp. The visitor first passed through a vaulted doorway, flanked by two square towers with battlements on top. The entrance was guarded by two colossal winged bulls with human heads, standing in profile facing the door; two more of these awesome creatures stood opposite each other on the inside of the door, with the result that those entering the palace always saw two the heads of two genies.

This gateway led into a vast quadrangle covering almost a quarter of an acre; this was the ceremonial courtyard, where great receptions were held. Around it were a number of large rooms, each of which had a door, usually flanked by colossal statues, opening on to the courtyard itself. It connected with other courtyards, which were all ringed by doors leading to

Entrance of a royal tomb, Ur.

rooms such as those we have just described; in all, there were about ten courtyards, big and small, and some sixty rooms. The walls were covered with alabaster panels, on which the king's accomplishments were glowingly depicted in the form of bas-reliefs. The floor was paved with brick tiles, which were covered with carpets; any part of the floor which was not carpeted, was paved with stone slabs bearing a carved design similar to the pattern of the carpets. This was the part of the palace where the men resided, and which was used for the reception of visitors. A seven-story pyramid devoted to the cult of the stars was situated in a corner of this section, next to a small temple.

Behind the men's quarters stood an isolated building, with high walls, which housed the women. Access to the two-acre site was possible only through two fortified gates. Here again, the rooms were arranged around a series of courtyards, the principal one had walls which were faced with enamelled bricks representing fantastic animals; huge painted statues stood at either side of the doors. Rows of columns formed an arcade which ran all around this courtyard and supported a gallery above; the general effect they produced on the visitor must have been that of a palm-grove, as each column was plated with a bronze bark and ended in a sheaf of gilded bronze palms.

The rest of the palace consisted of accommodation for servants, the kitchens, cellars, granaries, bakeries, stables, and also the *treasure room,* where gold and silver, together with anything seized as booty or offered as tribute, was stored.

In all, the palace had 208 rooms, of varying

Decorative work on south-east entrance of the palace of Sargon.

size. One thing they all had in common was that they were narrow; the length of the bigger ones, in particular, far exceeded their width, so that they looked more like tunnels than rooms. None of them had any windows, receiving all their air and light through a big door, sometimes 15 feet high, which opened into a courtyard. In this way, the people sought relief from the scorching sun.

Multi-storied temples

Chaldaean and Assyrian temples were shaped like tall, square towers, with seven floors. The palaces of all the kings of Assyria had one such temple; but the biggest ones were undoubtedly those of Babylon.

The ruin known as *Birs-Nimrud* still stands 200 feet high, higher than the towers of the Cathedral of Notre Dame in Paris. This ruin is what remains of the temple of Bel, each side of which measured 400 yards. In the middle, on an embankment which towered over the plain, stood the great tower, with sides measuring 200 yards; on it stood a similar but smaller tower, which, in turn, supported a third, smaller tower, and so on up to the seventh tower at the top of the whole structure.

Each of the seven towers in this tapering edifice was dedicated to one of the seven stars and was painted in that star's color; their order, from the bottom up, was as follows: white, black, purple, blue, vermilion, silver, gold. Access from one tower to the next was provided by an outside spiral staircase.

The last tower was crowned by a chapel containing a table made of gold, and a richly decorated bed; here, under a gilded cupola which shone brightly in the sun, a priest stood watch. The total height may have been as much as 550 feet.

The tower in the palace of Sargon has sides measuring 130 feet, each floor being 20 feet high.

Sculpture

The few Assyrian or Chaldaean statues that have been found are much less beautiful than Egyptian statues. For one thing, the whole region lacked suitable materials for sculpture: Assyrian stone is a kind of soft limestone, easily cut into thin layers, and thus excellent for bas-reliefs, but no good for statues. In Chaldaea, there is no stone at all. The statues found at Sirtella were made from black stone imported by sea; the people they depict are all standing or seated, are wearing long embroidered garments and have bare feet.

Assyrian sculptors specialized in bas-reliefs on large panels of alabaster or soft limestone, for the decoration of palace walls. The biggest panels were put on the outer walls; they represented colossal genies, genies with eagles' heads, giants strangling lions, or winged bulls with human faces. At Khorsabad, there were 26 pairs of winged bulls, between 12 and 15 feet high; they were carved on two faces, so as to give the impression that they were actually part of the wall. These bulls have five feet, with the result that, from one direction, they seem to have four feet, and, from the other, two. Their

Reconstruction of a Chaldaean temple.

Babylonian bas-relief, unrestored.

head is crowned with a tiara, and their hair is curled. They have a most unnerving stare. When entering the Assyrian room at the Louvre, in Paris, one cannot fail to be struck by the great power of these majestic monsters.

The bas-reliefs on the inner walls showed scenes from the life of the king who had been responsible for the building of the palace. Often arranged in strip-cartoon form, these sculptures were quite long; for example, a mile and a quarter of them were found at Khorsabad, while even greater lengths have been discovered at Calah and Nineveh.

This whole body of sculpture was executed in a matter of a few years. Many artists must have been engaged on it simultaneously, which might account for its very uneven standard. The battle scenes are amusing and instructive, because the

sculptor has shown everything in detail—the long lines of prisoners being led away, the corpses strewn over the battlefield, the trees on the mountainside, birds in their nests or on the branches of trees, the fish in the water. But usually the draftsmanship is pretty clumsy—almost, at times, the casual scribbling to be found on a schoolboy's exercise-book; the men are bigger than their horses, sometimes even bigger than the fortresses, the fish are as big as the ships, the vultures are easily as big as the corpse they are feeding on, and birds may be as tall as trees. Perspective, in other words, is lacking altogether. It was common for the artist to enlarge those persons who interested him the most: the king thereby becomes bigger than his ministers, and the Assyrians bigger than their enemies. The artists were unable to draw the full face, so that, whenever a figure had to be shown from the front, the face, like all the other faces in these bas-reliefs, was shown in profile. The faces are quite expressionless, neither laughing nor crying. The bodies are almost always concealed under heavy garments leaving only the head, hands and feet visible.

Nonetheless, there are some remarkable pieces; these are the great bas-reliefs depicting the king and his servants. They render in perfect detail the beards and the curled hair, the embroidery on the cloak and the crown, the silk fringe on the hem of a garment, etc. Sometimes one feels that the artist was executing a portrait.

The masterpieces of Assyrian art are the hunting dogs and wild animals. There is a bas-relief of Ashurbanipal out hunting which shows a lioness which has been struck by an arrow;

121

it is struggling to stand up on its front paws, roaring in pain, while its paralyzed hind-quarters are depicted with minute attention to detail. Even the Greeks could not represent animals more vividly than this.

Wounded lion . . . (Bas-relief from palace of Ashurbanipal; British Museum.).

The artist responsible for the decoration of a huge palace obviously could not hope to handle all the work himself. He had, under his command, a whole legion of subordinates whose work he supervised and to whom he entrusted only the less important tasks, reserving for himself the main scenes, that is, these in which the king himself appeared. He would not have wanted to entrust this task to an indifferent sculptor; but, in any case, the sovereign was anxious to see a true likeness of himself: *Sama bunaniya*, 'the image of my face', were the very words he used to use, and, naturally, the sculptor had to comply with the royal wish.

Animals are always rendered with special care; this being an area in which the artists of Nineveh achieved indisputable greatness. In the bas-reliefs of Ashur-na-sir-pal engaged in hunting, the animals are given rather sketchy treatment, as is the whole scene in general, and lose some of the finer qualities which an unclad figure requires, if a sense of movement and life is to be conveyed. At Nineveh, the artist achieved extraordinary realism, particularly in the bas-reliefs of Ashurbanipal, whether it be the dogs straining at the leash, herds of cattle, sheep or goats, or further on, the mule carrying heavy bags or the horse striding into battle. Horses in battle, in fact, seem to have had a particular appeal for Assyrian sculptors.

The potter's art: some very early specimens.
(Louvre; Abassid Museum, Baghdad).

*Detail from a bas-relief, Nimrud. Right: crystal
tablet, about 700 B.C. (Baghdad Museum).*

Left: head of a person, bas-relief from Nimrud (very early work). Above:
The Hammurabi law.

Cuneiform characters on brick structure. Right: inscription on a bas-relief.

Ornamentation

The bricks used in the walls of the palaces were entirely hidden by a layer of white stucco on which decorative frescoes were painted, or by a layer of enamelled bricks portraying human figures.

The technique involved drawing a part of the total picture on each brick, then applying the colored enamel and, finally, baking the brick. Bricks enamelled in this way were then grouped together in order to form a complete figure. These brightly colored bricks produced a very brilliant over-all effect.

Graphic ornamentation, on flagstones or enamelled bricks, carpets or garments, usually depicted plants, fantastic animals or simply patterns of lines. Festoons, palmettes, rosettes, griffons, flourishes and virtually all the types of ornamentation used in the East and imitated by us in the West, all came to us from the Chaldaeans.

Cuneiform script

More than three thousand years before the Christian era, the Chaldaeans knew how to write, as can be seen from the inscriptions which have been found in all the cities of Chaldaea and Assyria, even the oldest of them.

Most of the inscriptions are imprinted on baked bricks of different forms, some of them being flat tablets, others looking like cakes of toilet soap, while others look rather like miniature barrels. The inscriptions were made with a metal stylus with a flat triangular tip, with

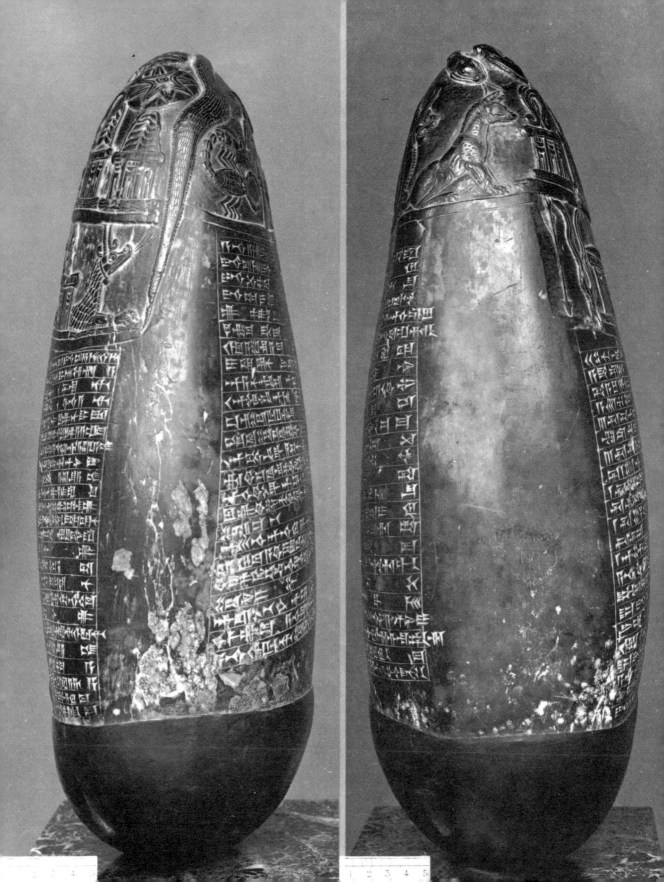

Left: a rather curious "pebble" (about 1,100 B.C.), with decorative work
and carved inscriptions. It stands 1 ft. 8 ins. high. (Paris, Bibliothèque
Nationale). Above: bas-relief, Nimrud.

Assyrian ornamental themes,
taken from bas-reliefs.

which marks were made in the clay while it was still wet. The marks thus produced all looked like elongated triangles, and have been compared to arrows or wedges; for this reason, scholars named this form of writing *cuneiform* (from the Latin word *cuneus,* wedge). Once the inscription was completed, the clay was baked hard in an oven, thereby making a permanent impression. The entire contents of the library found in the palace of Ashurbanipal consists of baked brick tablets covered with script on both sides.

This system served to render in print not only the Chaldaean and Assyrian languages, but also the languages of all neighboring peoples: Susian, Armenian, Cappadocian, Median and Persian.

The Chaldaean and Assyrian script was exceedingly complicated. Each character was made up of a combination of several wedge-shaped strokes. In ancient times one character represented a single word (for example, sun,

moon, fish); later, certain characters were taken to represent a syllable (*ba, bi, ga, la, lum, kat),* and it was these *syllabic* characters that were used to write the majority of words.

However, there were more than two hundred syllabic characters, most of which looked very much alike and were easily confused. Moreover, a number of the older characters, which represented a word, had also been kept in use, so that, in some instances, the same character served to designate a whole word and, at the same time, one syllable. Worse still, there were some characters which could be read in two quite different ways: for example, *an* and *ilu.*

This was certainly a very difficult script, even for the Chaldaeans themselves. In order to use it properly, they needed special books, vocabularies, grammars, and dictionaries, some of which have been of great help to modern scholars in their deciphering of other cuneiform texts.

Cuneiform script seems to have originated in Chaldaea, some time before the period known as the *Semitic occupation.* From there, it spread into Asia, where it underwent numerous transformations, depending on the place and the period.

The formation of these characters on the brick was an easy matter, as ancient calligraphers have shown in the handiwork they left behind. They wrote on the wet clay with a *stylus,* some samples of which have been found; then, when the tablet was covered with script, they wisely baked it solid, so as to make it indelible. Their *books* thus defied the elements, and were able to withstand water, and fire, and were spared the slow process of erosion by time the passage of time and also brutal destruction by man.

Books were kept in rows in huge libraries, where scholars came to copy them for the libraries of the Assyrian palaces.

The room in the palace of Ashurbanipal which contains what has come to be known as the *Nineveh library,* contains a large number of historical narratives, as well as tablets containi describing various ancient legends, such as the account of the *Chaldaean Genesis,* the *Epic of Gilgamish,* which gives a curious Chaldaean version of the Flood, and also a number of documents dealing with Magic, Divination, and the interpretation of omens. There are other documents on science, medicine, astronomy and natural history.

Other tablets mention eclipses of the sun, observations on the planets and the fixed stars, and also the determination of the period of the equinoxes. Some of them contain a vast amount of useful information on natural history, the classification of animals, insects, plants, minerals, and also precise instructions on the construction of houses, temples and ships.

One series of tablets is devoted to agriculture. The farmer was told when would be the most suitable time for plowing, sowing and reaping; how he should till the soil, water it, remove the weeds and ensure a good yield at harvest-time. An account is given of which animals should be considered as pests, and which, one the contrary, should be protected.

The tablets in the Nineveh library were arranged very systematically on shelves, together with special indications to help the reader consult them more easily.

Ramparts and one of the gates of Babylon (reconstruction).

Cuneiform characters have often been compared to nails . . . Right: a new kind of art—though a not particularly original kind—was about to flourish in Assyria. This bust of the Sassanid King Sapor Ii (303–379) is an illustration of it.

One industry in Babylon which was very much an art was that of making engraved stones; as we learn from Herodotus, every Babylonian had his own seal, in the form of a cylinder made of hard stones, such as jasper, cornelian, sard, and, above all, hematite. Special emblems were also carved on their walking-sticks, which, as it were, established the identity of the person.

Following pages: statuettes of Babylonian women, . . . Greek style. The last page of the great Assyrian epic has been turned. (Louvre).

While Assyrian sculptors modelled their works on nature as much as they could, the enamellers, on the other hand, concentrated solely on decoration, and on the brilliant interplay and contrast of colors with which to delight the eye. For them, figures were a mere pretext; they enoyed enjoyed a greater freedom when working with plant shapes, which lent themselves more readily to fantastic treatment; for them, leaves and flowers had an infinite potential as a source of curves and straight lines—as geometric figures which the artist transformed into rosettes, squares and diamond-shapes.

141